A NATURAL BATTLEGROUND
Bobbie Oliver

Red Swan Series Vol 1

First published in 2019 by Interventions Inc

Interventions is a not-for-profit, independent left wing book publisher.
For further information:
    www.interventions.org.au
    interventionspublications@gmail.com
    Trades Hall Suite 68
    54 Victoria Street
    Carlton VIC 3053

Design and layout by Viktoria Ivanova

Series Editor: Alexis Vassiley

Author: Oliver, Bobbie

Title: A Natural Battleground: The fight to establish a rail heritage centre at Western Australia's Midland Railway Workshops

ISBN(s): 978-0-9945378-4-3 : Paperback

© Bobbie Oliver 2019

The moral rights of the author have been asserted

All rights reserved. Except as permitted under the Australian Copyright Act 1968 (for example, a fair dealing for the purposes of study, research, criticism or review), no part of this book may be reproduced, stored in a retrieval system, communicated or transmitted in any form or by any means without prior written permission.

All inquiries should be made to the author.

 A catalogue record for this book is available from the National Library of Australia

A NATURAL BATTLEGROUND

The fight to establish a rail heritage centre at Western Australia's Midland Railway Workshops

Bobbie Oliver

INTERVENTIONS
MELBOURNE

ACKNOWLEDGEMENTS

Earlier versions of several chapters appeared in peer refereed conference proceedings published by the Society for the Study of Labour History (2003, 2005), the British World Conference, Melbourne (2004) and *State of Australian Cities, National Conference Perth* (2009). The photographs are individually acknowledged in the captions. Those marked as being 'courtesy of the Midland Railway Workshops History Project' were donated to the project by individuals, but the photographer is unknown. I thank Neil Byrne (President, Labour History Society) who has never ceased fighting for a Rail Heritage Centre at the Midland Workshops; the University of Western Australia for offering me an Honorary Research Fellowship; my former researcher Linley Batterham, who compiled the statistics on accidents and fatalities discussed in Chapter 2; Alexis Vassiley for introducing me to Interventions; the readers who recommended publication, and my editor Janey Stone and other staff at Interventions for their dedicated and competent work in producing *A Natural Battleground*; and Sandra Goldbloom Zurbo for copy editing. Without them, this book may never have eventuated.

CONTENTS

	Introduction	1
1	It's more than just the buildings; it's what they did inside	5
2	Interpreting Workers' Space	25
3	Midland Workshops as a Site of the British Diaspora	35
4	Midland Railway Workshops: A site of initiation	47
5	Political Activity at the Midland Railway Workshops	59
6	Technological Change at the Workshops, 1960s–1990s	73
7	Midland Railway Workshops: A history lesson?	85
8	What now?	101
	Endnotes	109
	Bibliography	119
	Index	127

INTRODUCTION

More than just locomotives

The Western Australian Government Railways (WAGR) Workshops at Midland, east of Perth, was once the state's largest employer of skilled tradesmen, and trained the most trades apprentices. At its peak in the 1950s, the Workshops had over 3000 employees, including 557 apprentices. In his memoir, Ron Wadham, who was works manager from 1978 to 1989, somewhat cynically summarised industrial relations: 'Managers are appointed to screw the workers. Trade unions are out to screw the management. In between is a grey area where a working compromise is achieved.' Consequently, he wrote, 'The Railway Workshops was a natural battleground. Management working within general guidelines and trade unions taking what action they could to test the limits of management's discretionary powers and gain better working conditions for their members.' Management, unions and workers are long gone, but in the twenty-first century the site remains a battleground. Now the battle is between those who want to preserve its history by including a rail heritage museum in the site plan, and those who, in their desire for profit, seem to want to forget history.

The Workshops closed on 4 March 1994. For several years, after the site was stripped of any useful machinery, the magnificent buildings stood idle while various interested parties argued about what to do with them. Meanwhile, much of the state's heavy manufacturing went interstate as Western Australia's private firms revealed their lack of capacity to take over the Workshops' role that they had so avidly coveted while it was still operational.

In 1998, as a member of the Perth branch of the Australian Society for the Study of Labour History (hereafter the Labour History Society), I attended a meeting to discuss collecting the history before the buildings were demolished. Former employees didn't talk of the technology, or even about the locomotives that were built there. They didn't see the place as the site where particularly iconic locomotives were built, even though it was the workers' proud boast that at the Workshops they made everything needed to maintain Western Australia's rail network, from the dogspikes that held the rails to the sleepers, to bridge girders and the largest of locomotive engine parts, including the boilers. In particular, they wanted the society to collect the workers' stories, not only about their skills – of which they were justly proud – but also a narrative of their struggles with the management, their dangerous working conditions, their humour, their anecdotes, the characters, and the ways they bent and broke the rules. There was a very strong sense of place among former workers. As will be shown in the chapters, the factory floor was a place of conflict between bosses and workers (a natural battleground in their eyes, too). Former employees seemed eager to show how they subverted an autocratic system in which they had no power.

With colleagues from Curtin and Murdoch Universities, I was successful in obtaining two Australia Research Council (ARC) Linkage grants over a five-year period (2000–04 inclusive), to administer a project that would yield books, including a major history, scholarly papers, some of which are partially reproduced here, electronic resources, and oral, photographic and documentary archives. By a decade after the Workshops closed, we had made considerable progress in conserving the site and preserving its history. The decision to preserve many of the buildings was facilitated by the state branch of the Australian Labor Party (ALP) being elected to government in 2001. Premier Geoff Gallop's uncle had been a foreman boilermaker in the Workshops' boiler shop, which gave him a personal connection to the place. There were many other personal and union links between ALP members past and present and the Workshops. Furthermore, the people of Midland, with assistance from the Labour History Society, made it clear that they wanted public facilities, including a rail heritage centre, on the site.

From 2005 until 2008, the refurbished timekeeper's office housed an Interpretive Centre, where visitors could view artefacts and watch a documentary history of the Workshops, retold by former employees.

Next door to the Interpretive Centre, the Midland Redevelopment Authority (MRA), which was responsible for site, constructed a Workers Wall (inspired by a wall in the STEAM Museum at Swindon in Britain), with each brick bearing the name and trade or role of a Workshops employee.

Yet the project's hope of interpreting the workers' stories *in situ* in a purpose-built facility inside one of the major buildings has not eventuated. In the years since the Interpretation Centre was closed, the MRA's successor, the Metropolitan Redevelopment Authority (MetRA), which now has charge of the site, has taken steps to remove much of the internal fabric, although the main buildings remain under heritage protection.

This book is based on a revised collection of papers that I presented at various conferences throughout the project's duration and afterwards. Some are derived from spoken papers, others published as written papers and adapted and reproduced here with the kind permission of the sources named in the acknowledgements. In order to bring the story up to date as at the end of 2018, some new material has been included. The book's main aim is to emphasise the importance of preserving industrial worksites in general and this worksite in particular. The following chapters discuss the context and organisation of the Midland Workshops History Project (1998–2004), the challenges faced in interpreting an industrial heritage site, arguments for the Workshops' significance in Australian industrial and labour history, and reasons why attempts to establish a rail heritage centre have failed. I hope that this is not the end of the story and that this book will inspire others to raise the Workshops' proud history from its present doldrums and find resources for its meaningful interpretation on the site.

1
It's more than just the buildings; it's what they did inside

Industrial worksites are not everyone's idea of a beautiful landscape, which is why, once they cease to function, they are usually demolished and the land reclaimed for more aesthetic purposes. The East Perth redevelopment is one example of a landscape from which the industrial past has been obliterated. Yet to those who worked there, that place is vested with a particular significance. In recent decades, communities around the world have come to recognise the significance of place to individuals and groups. The *Australia ICOMOS [International Council on Monuments and Sites] Charter of Places of Cultural Significance* (1979), known as the *Burra Charter*, states: 'Many places are important to us because they tell us about who we are and the past that has formed us.'

Using the example of the Western Australian Government Railways (WAGR) Workshops, located in the Perth suburb of Midland and declared a state heritage icon in 2004, I argue that there is significant social and historical value in retaining and re-using industrial sites, while appropriately and sensitively interpreting their past. Industrial sites often contain substantial brick buildings, exemplified in this discussion by the three main blocks at the Midland Workshops. These sites are testimony to an era when thousands of workers produced manufactured goods for domestic use and export. In the pre-diesel era, the Workshops produced all the components for an entire state railway system, including steam locomotives and rolling stock, rails, bridge girders and small items such as the dogspikes used to fix rails to sleepers.

This chapter's title is taken from lines in a song that Fremantle musician and folk singer Bernard Carney composed for the Workshops History Project in 2000: 'We talk about our heritage, it cannot be denied / It's more than just the buildings; it's what they did inside.' Major workshop sites hold significance for thousands of working people, shaping their lives and defining them as individuals. Arguably, such significant industrial heritage might be retained on the grounds that it is collective heritage. Geographer Graeme Aplin posits that a European gothic cathedral is part of the collective heritage of Western civilisation. Should cathedrals of industry be similarly treasured? Are the Midland Workshops part of Western Australia's, Australia's or even the world's collective heritage?

To answer these questions, this chapter commences with an assessment of the significance of the Midland Workshops in Western Australia's industrial history. It then discusses the closure of the Workshops, and the research project established in 1998 to record the site's history. Using examples of workshop interpretation from elsewhere in Australia and the United Kingdom, I compare these with what was achieved at Midland. I conclude that the Midland Workshops are of sufficient social, scientific and industrial value to be regarded as a part of Western Australia's and Australia's collective heritage. The site also has heritage significance for the countries of the former British Empire in that it is an example of the diaspora of skilled British tradesmen in the twentieth century (see also chapter 3).

Significance

Article 6 of the *Burra Charter* states: 'Understanding the cultural significance of a place is the first major stage of a conservation project.' The following outline establishes the context of the Midland Workshops and their significance for the city of Perth and the state of Western Australia. In 1904, the WAGR Workshops was relocated from the port of Fremantle to a 260 acre (105.2 hectare) site at Midland Junction, 19 kilometres east of Perth. Midland Junction was where the private railways of the Midland Railway Company (heading north to Geraldton) and the Canning Timber Company in the Perth hills joined the government railway system. Already the location of several government instrumentalities and small industries, Midland enjoyed a brief boom when the WAGR Workshops was established, after which the population settled at around 5000 for much of the first half of the

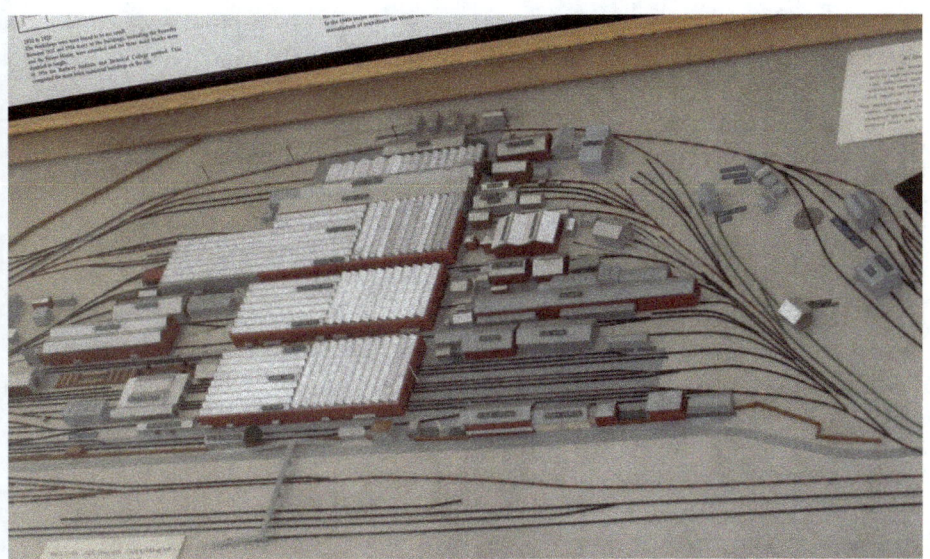

Scale model of the Workshops, showing (bottom to top) Blocks 1, 2 and 3 (Block 3 with Munitions Annexe extension on the left end). The long building on the right of Block 2 is the foundry. Near the bottom right of Block 1 are the timekeeper's office, the gatehouse, the Peace Memorial and the CME's office. (Photo courtesy of Bobbie Oliver)

twentieth century. Further commercial and industrial development occurred in the 1950s and 1960s, but Midland was not regarded as a desirable residential address because of the presence of heavy industry and its image as a railway town.

For much of their ninety-year history (1904–94) the Workshops was the largest industrial employer in Western Australia, employing a workforce of between 1000 and 3500, including up to 500 trades apprentices. Employees proudly boasted that the Workshops manufactured everything required to maintain and run the state's rail network. As rail historian Philippa Rogers has stated:

> From the smallest split pin to the largest locomotive, from the window blinds to the full carriage, from a dogspike to a compound turnout, from a brake block to a modern, aluminium wagon … from a cupboard to a fully equipped trainmen's barracks and so much more, the Midland Workshops was an integral part of the WAGR rail system … Without the railway system, the Workshops would have had little reason for being, but without the Workshops, the railway system could not have existed.

Apart from manufacturing and repairing railway engines and rolling stock, the Workshops made munitions during World War II. A thorough apprenticeship training equipped graduating tradesmen for work around Australia and beyond in many industries, including the railways, power stations, carpentry, marine engineering, mining and lecturing in technical colleges. Three former junior workers rose through the ranks to become chief mechanical engineer, thus demonstrating the value the WAGR placed on shop floor training as a basis for an engineering career. Many recalled their apprenticeship days with pride. By the 1980s, however, changes in technology, combined with the increased use of road transport and privatisation of industries, led to a reduction in the workforce. The Workshops closed on 4 March 1994.

Since 2000, the Workshops site has been managed first by the Midland Redevelopment Authority (MRA) and latterly by the Metropolitan Redevelopment Authority (also MRA but to avoid confusion MetRA is used to distinguish the latter organisation). In 2001, the site was assessed by the Heritage Council of Western Australia as 'represent[ing] the most significant example of an early twentieth century railway Workshop in Australia'; it was 'the most substantial industrial complex established by the WA Government at the beginning of the twentieth century'. The Workshops 'played a major role in the economy, development and daily life of Western Australians for ninety years, including training thousands of apprentices in a wide range of trades'. Many of the buildings were assessed as having individual value, and the site contained 'a wide range of significant machinery, much of which remains operable, and collections of tools, equipment, furniture and fittings'.

Eight buildings, all constructed by 1904, were identified as having exceptional heritage significance: the three main blocks and later additions such as the flagpole and the peace memorial, the chief mechanical engineer (CME)'s office, the Railway Institute building, the pattern shop, the power house, and the old tarpaulin shop. Other buildings, including the foundry and the timekeeper's office (built 1924), are regarded as being of 'considerable significance'. In addition, the heritage architects, Heritage and Conservation Professionals, recommended the pattern shop, the power house, the timekeeper's office and Block 1 for reuse as a rail heritage centre.

Prior to this assessment moves had already begun to record the site's history. The Labour History Society organised the site's first Open Day on 21 March 1999. It had taken months to obtain government permission to enter the site, because authorities claimed that it was too dangerous to admit the general public. Finally, the Technical and Further Education (TAFE) college on site granted permission to stage an exhibition on their premises in the former CME's office building. The Society held a photographic exhibition and arranged strictly supervised tours, conducted by former Workshops employees, around parts of Blocks 1, 2 and 3. The restrictions included refusing people entry to the site if they were not wearing covered footwear; many people were disappointed; they were turned away because they were wearing sandals.

At that first open day, the organisers expected a few hundred people; 3000 came. This pattern continued throughout the early 2000s, when the MRA held annual open days, at which the Labour History Society staged exhibitions of the work of the history project (discussed below) and signed up former Workshops employees for interviews. The site continued to attract and fascinate not only past employees but also their children, their grandchildren and the general public. In 2002, when Open Day was combined with Premier Geoff Gallop's opening of the new Helena Street level crossing linking the Workshops site to the Midland city centre, an estimated 80,000 people came to the city centre and the Workshops.

The Workshops History Project

From 1998, the Workshops was the subject of an extensive history project, begun by the Labour History Society. The history project was developed on seven principles:

1. collaboration between trained academic historians, union officials, and past employees
2. the interviews, ephemera, documents, and photographs collected would be lodged in archives, so as to be accessible to researchers
3. the establishment of appropriate collecting and documentation protocols
4. prioritising workers' own stories, although the project aimed to educate the wider public about factory working conditions and processes, the skills required by trades people and the objects of their production, as well as social aspects of the lives of factory workers and their families

5   the project would largely depend upon volunteers
6   adequate training and support for volunteers in their tasks of interviewing, transcribing tapes, and collecting material meant that the project would teach skills to members of the community
7   the project would be a vehicle for informed debate about the preservation of the site and of industrial heritage in general.

In 2000, fellow Curtin University historian Dr Patrick Bertola and I obtained an Australian Research Council (ARC) grant for $80,000 over two years, matched with $80,000 cash and in kind from six industry partners. With funds from this grant, the history project employed a manger, Ric McCracken, to contact past Workshops employees and embark on a program of training volunteers to undertake interviews. The J. S. Battye Library of Western Australian History (hereafter the Battye Library) assisted with setting up protocols and documentation for collecting and cataloguing taped interviews, photographs and private papers. Together with Murdoch University media lecturers Mia Lindgren and Brogan Bunt, and a further five industry partners added to the original team, we obtained a second, much larger grant in 2001, that would enable us to collect more research material and to publish a major history and electronic resources about the Workshops.

By mid 2002, when the first grant was acquitted, the project had compiled a register of over 200 past employees who were willing to be interviewed. A survey form, filled out by the contributors, provided a source of information upon which to base relevant interview questions. The project recruited a team of six volunteers, who proved to be excellent interviewers, transcribers and researchers. Along with Murdoch and Curtin University students, they undertook the majority of the 200 plus hours of taped interviews that were lodged with the Battye Library and the Local History section of the Midland Library by the project's completion in December 2004. Interviewees also donated photographs, memoirs, poetry, documents such as trade certificates and union books, and objects (tool boxes, a typewriter, 'foreigners' – objects that workers made unofficially in the Workshops and secretly removed from the premises for private use, or sometimes for profit – sports shields, badges and so forth). Documents and photographs donated to the project are now lodged with the Battye Library in the Midland Workshops History Project collection, MN 2758; Acc. no. 7625A. The interviews are catalogued separately under individual names of interviewees and/or interviewers. These objects were included in exhibitions on Workshops Open Days and in the Midland Library. The most successful, *Under the Lap, Over the Fence: Foreigner Production at the Midland Workshops*, an exhibition of foreigners, was staged in the foundry at the 2004 open day and formed the basis for *Foreigners: Secret Artefacts of Industrialism*, a book, edited by the exhibition's curator, Dr Jennifer Harris. The displays informed people about the project and disseminated information about the people, skills and processes of the Workshops.

By mid 2009, the project had produced a DVD, a web page, a major researched history of the Workshops that won the 2006 Premier's Literary Award for Western Australian History, two other published books, and numerous conference papers, chapters and electronic media. Many of these are listed in the Sources at the end of this book. Murdoch student Simone McGurk (now Labor MLA for the state seat of Fremantle) won the Best Radio Feature Award at Murdoch University's Radio and Film Awards, 2002, for her program on the visit of American singer Paul Robeson to the Midland Workshops in December 1960. Students at Murdoch and Curtin Universities wrote research essays and interviewed former employees as part of their history, heritage or media studies assignments.

While the history project's aims did not include the establishment of a rail heritage centre on the site, the seventh principle indicated that we intended to work for the preservation of the site with its heritage objects remaining *in situ*. We strongly believed that the interviews, documents and artefacts that the project collected should be preserved in Midland for the people of Midland. When the idea of a local rail heritage centre was tested with a survey, the Midland public responded enthusiastically. Hundreds signed a letter to the MRA, requesting the establishment of a rail heritage centre or museum. This would have involved either creating a purpose-built facility or adapting part of the existing buildings on the Workshops site. The latter course was our preference.

Regrettably, industrial history and heritage have not attracted very many advocates for their conservation in Australia. Almost three decades ago, in the context of a debate over the demolition of the finger wharf at Woolloomooloo (NSW), Peter Spearritt reminded us that

> The conservation of industrial heritage is determined primarily by taste and money rather than by historical importance or cultural significance... Most professional historians in Australia do not want to say this before

any commission of inquiry or court hearing for the simple reason that taste is much harder to define than historical significance and historians have not to date claimed much expertise in the matter of taste.

This attitude has certainly been evident in Western Australia. Before the Workshops History Project began in 1998, the Midland Workshops – despite being Perth's largest industrial site – had been almost completely ignored by scholars. The history project happened because unionists who had worked at the site approached the Labour History Society to contact and interview past employees and try to capture the site's history before it was too late. They had the right idea. The planning and creation of a heritage centre in the Midland Workshops required input from labour historians in particular, to ensure effective presentation and interpretation of the relationship between history and heritage. Because of their training and skills, historians must have a central role in any heritage conservation and interpretation project.

From small beginnings, the project developed into a major research and teaching resource, generating the range of academic and student outcomes detailed above. It was also the model for a similar research project involving another of Perth's major industrial sites, the East Perth Power Station, which operated from 1916 until its closure in 1981. The material that the Workshops History Project unearthed gave its historians the confidence to advise the heritage architects and, on occasions, to make a point of insisting on the significance of particular buildings or the retention or location of artefacts, fittings or equipment. The discipline of historical scholarship provides the tools to analyse and interpret the social and political significance of a site. Too often, historians have been regarded as merely adjuncts in heritage conservation and interpretation. Architects have been granted precedence because heritage is often regarded as being just buildings. Yet, as Bernard Carney reminded us, it's as much about what went on in the buildings as the buildings themselves.

Public authorities also have an essential role to play. By 1998, the Workshops had been closed for four years. It was impossible to gain access to the site until months of negotiation had occurred between the Labour History Society and the state government. Over the duration of the history project, access became available on a daily basis, largely because project staff established a good working relationship with the MRA. This was achieved by adopting several strategies.

Developing strategic partnerships

We set about forming strategic partnerships. First, although much of the project was carried out by volunteers and students, our project manager Ric McCracken liaised and created networks with our industry partners and with the institutions directly involved with the site, such as the City of Swan and the MRA. Naturally enough, a public authority reflects the wishes and intentions of its relevant government minister, which can be a weakness and a strength. In 2000, the history project's first funded year, the politically conservative Liberal–National Party coalition led by Premier Richard Court was still in government. Graham Kierath, who held the portfolios of Planning and Heritage, was much more oriented to redevelopment than to conservation. Initially, the MRA Board contained no historical or heritage expertise. In March 2000, the historic munitions annexe, which extended from the eastern end of Block 3, was demolished to make way for a road into the new police complex on the eastern end of the site. The annexe had been omitted from the Heritage Council's curtilage because of lack of information about its significance. Despite a campaign by members of the Labour History Society, which included funding a researcher to provide further information about the building's significance, the Heritage Council would not reconsider their decision. Thus the state's last intact building connected with munitions production in World War II was demolished.

In February 2001, the ALP, led by Dr Geoff Gallop, was elected to government. Because of the ALP's industrial roots, and the existence of personal connections between the Workshops and some Labor members of parliament (including the premier), the new administration indicated to the MRA that priorities at the site would change. This considerably assisted the history project. As shown above, the MRA agreed to become an industry partner in the ARC Linkage grant that Dr Patrick Bertola and I secured at the beginning of 2002. So, too, did the local authority, the City of Swan.

Further lobbying to the new Heritage Minister, Alannah McTiernan, resulted in a state rail heritage forum, which the MRA hosted in their new offices in the restored Railway Institute building on 8 June 2002. The forum brought together a number of key groups interested in the site from labour history, machinery preservation or railway heritage perspectives. Their comments indicated the extent to which many groups wanted to see a rail heritage centre on the Midland Workshops site, the preparedness of groups to work together to achieve aims, and the need for a strategy that would outline feasibility and funding options to put before the state government. There was never again such a propitious time for action.

Following the Forum, Ric McCracken wrote a paper entitled 'Planning for a State Rail Heritage Centre at the Midland Workshops', which was submitted to the MRA. This paper proposed the development of a strategic plan to define the scope of, and opportunities represented by, a state rail heritage centre in the Workshops. It emphasised the need for such a plan to address

> The active restoration of rolling stock and locos, working machinery indicative of the skills practiced in the Workshops over the 90 year history of its operation, [and] an interpretative centre which collects and presents the oral histories of former employees, family members and the community with informative and interpretative ephemera and memorabilia, important and iconic areas of the site such as the peace memorial and gardens, the flagpole and the assembly area around it and other signifiers of activities [e.g. grapevines].

In addition, heritage architects Heritage and Conservation Professionals' *Heritage Strategy for the Midland Central Redevelopment Area* (hereafter *Heritage Strategy*), recommended the pattern shop, the power house, the timekeeper's office and Block 1 for reuse as a rail heritage centre.

It was also necessary to have the support of other public authorities, in particular the Western Australian Museum. The expertise of museum staff in managing large projects and premises, conserving material objects and creating exhibitions was needed if we were to achieve a heritage centre at the Workshops site. The museum was interested in working in partnership with the MRA. As just one example of how this expertise manifested itself, it was pointed out that soil pollution from various industrial processes was a major problem of the site. An expert at the museum suggested that this negative could be turned to a positive by using polluted areas to demonstrate new technological processes for removing pollutants. Had the MRA adopted this suggestion, part of the Workshops site could have become a test site for such processes, adding to knowledge and creating a cleaner environment. This did not happen, although considerable government funds were invested in removing contaminated top soil from the site, a process that resulted in the Interpretative Centre being closed in 2008; it was never reopened. A decade later, in mid 2018, the site of the Interpretive Centre, the timekeeper's office, stood vacant, with a 'To Let' sign advertising it as a site for a café. It is hard to see how a café could serve as an introductory site to the Workshops, as most of the floor space (once devoted to display cabinets) would be occupied by tables and chairs.

Preserving the site

From the beginning of the history project's second stage in February 2002, we worked closely with the MRA to achieve the preservation and appropriate interpretation of the site, so that the industrial heritage would not be lost. The research and published outcomes of the project were made available to the MRA as part of the partnership agreement and were used in the interpretive centre from 2005 until its closure in 2008.

Prior to this, the project had actively lobbied for a repository on the site. In February 2001, we hosted a visit by Associate Professor Lucy Taksa, of the University of New South Wales. Taksa addressed a public gathering of about 100 people at the Midland Town Hall and met with project volunteers and members of the MRA. In her address, she warned that

> Efforts to preserve our industrial past and our railway history and to celebrate them have been extremely limited. We have no equivalent to the Ironbridge Gorge museum in the United Kingdom or the Boot Cotton Mills at the Lowell Historical National Park in the United States. Nor do we have railway museums like the ones in York and Swindon in the United Kingdom ... While we still have our major railway workshops, at least in Midland, Sydney, Launceston and Ipswich, relatively few people have recognised their significance. At present all are facing varying degrees of redevelopment and reuse.

More recently, Canadian historian Steven High wrote of the reluctance to preserve industrial heritage sites in North America, asking, 'Whose history was worth preserving?' He pointed out that in Toronto, the move to preserve sites focused on 'the aesthetic value' exemplified by 'the homes and businesses of the wealthy' and 'civic buildings such as Toronto's Old City Hall, and Union Station ... Yet mills and factories ... were rarely seen as being worthy of preservation.' High stated that industrial buildings in the United States and Canada were either demolished or converted into 'condominiums, nightclubs or studios for artists'. Few retained any hint of their industrial past.

One imaginative reuse of a massive industrial site occurred at the Bethlehem Steel Works in Pennsylvania, a site far bigger than the Midland Railway Workshops, which once employed 30,000 workers, ten times the Midland workforce. As at Midland, soil contamination was a problem, prompting a 'mixed-usage plan' consisting of 'an industrial and office park, a high technology district, an entertainment complex, retail stores, and a *new Smithsonian-affiliated museum dedicated to America's industrial history*' (my emphasis). The plan included retaining 'the blast furnaces and other signature structures'. The National Museum of Industrial History opened in Bethlehem, Pennsylvania, in November 2016. One of its exhibits is a massive drop hammer, similar to the one

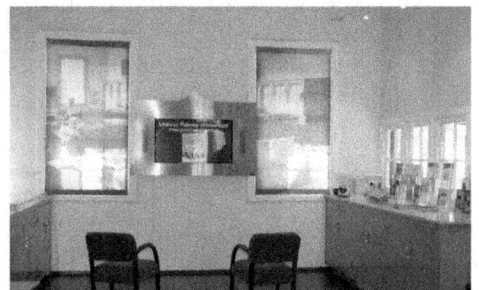

An Interpretive Centre opened in the refurbished timekeeper's office in 2005. Interior displays included videos produced by the Workshops History Project, artefacts and enlarged photographs on the window blinds depicting scenes of Workshops life. (Photo courtesy of Bobbie Oliver)

still *in situ* at the Midland Railway Workshops.

Demolition or drastic conversion appears the more likely fate for various parts of the Midland Railway Workshops site. High observed that, despite exceptions such as the Bethlehem Steel Mills site, where factories had been preserved, they were 'typically picturesque stone mills located in small towns and rural areas'. At the Midland Workshops, all the main buildings have been granted heritage status and are likely to be converted to suit a range of uses, none of them historical. So far, medical centres (partially put in place), a university campus, a hospital, light industry and even upper storey apartments above boutique businesses have all been suggested uses. The parts deemed to be of little or no historical or heritage importance have been demolished, among them the historic World War II Shell Munitions Annexe, the original computer building and a toilet block.

In her 2001 address, Lucy Taksa made several recommendations that served as useful guidelines for the establishment of a successful heritage centre at the Workshops; these guidelines were in sync with the project's principles. Taksa advocated the active involvement of community members, particularly former employees, and their 'visible presence' in the site's redevelopment and reuse. The importance of this type of collaboration could not be overemphasised in a project that depended upon strong community support. Past employees contributed an impressive range of skills and knowledge about processes and machinery at the Workshops, as well as a fund of stories that recreated the human dimensions of working there. Taksa compared institutions such as Pennsylvania's Altoona Railroaders Memorial Museum, which concentrated on 'collecting, preserving and interpreting objects', with Swindon's STEAM Museum, which identified the workers instead of celebrating their achievements in an anonymous, unacknowledged manner.

The Workshops History Project aimed to guide any museum or heritage centre developed at Midland into the latter category. A method employed at Swindon, a Wall of Names, has inspired similar projects at Eveleigh Workshops in Sydney and at Midland. The MRA, enthusiastically embracing the idea of a workers' wall, built a series of impressive brick and iron panels at the side of Block 1, on the newly named Yelverton Street (formerly Montreal Street East). For $25, past employees or their relatives could purchase a brick inscribed with the employee's name and occupation. Once it was engraved, the brick was then placed in one of the panels. The project was immediately popular with the public; however, this type of memorial should not be seen as a substitute for the appropriate restoration and use of buildings. The workers' wall in isolation means very little; surrounded by buildings and objects that still retain evidence of their original use, it has great significance.

Principle 3 in the *Heritage Strategy* (2001) stated that 'all site features of exceptional significance and considerable significance [should] be retained and preserved', and Principle 6, that 'areas of exceptional or considerable significance should be retained as open space'. Using these principles as a guide, it ought to be possible to walk through the redeveloped site and recognise the former use of the buildings; the streetscape should not be significantly altered.

Interpreting the site

Any work site is a place of many stories. How can those stories be preserved in the public domain, so that they remain evident in the fabric and purposes of the site? The History Project aimed to let the workers tell their own stories and to then include these in site interpretations. A few examples are used here to illustrate the richness of the material that was unearthed during the project's life. An area in Block 3, where a row of lathes used to stand, was known by the workers as 'Red Square'. There, active communist Jack Marks and some fellow Party members occupied a group of lathes. During their lunch break, in full view of the foreman's office, they would disseminate communist propaganda to anyone who was interested in listening. It was done as much to thumb the nose at authority (in the person of the foreman) as to make converts to communism. Chapter 5 describes in greater detail the significance of political activity at the Workshops and the challenges in interpreting it.

The flagpole outside Block 1 was famed as a workers' gathering point. Stop work meetings took place there, and political and industrial speeches were made at the flagpole, overlooked by the CME's office, referred to by the workers as 'Bullshit Castle'. In the minds of many employees, the flagpole was the focal point of the Workshops, although it had nothing to do with the technological processes of the site. Built as temporary memorial to Workshops employees who had served and been killed in World War I, prior to the construction of the permanent peace memorial in 1925, the flagpole became central to issues of industrial management and conciliation and arbitration. It was a space that the

View of the Shop Floor at the STEAM Museum, Swindon, UK, 2003, where the machines are still in use. (Photo courtesy of Bobbie Oliver)

workers claimed for themselves – their gathering point where they exercised the rights won for them by their unions. But it was also the site where, in April 1993, the workers learnt of the Workshops' closure. And, conversely, it was a site of boss–worker cooperation. Flagpole meetings were permitted during the lunch hour, and the management provided amplification for the speakers, fitted by an electrician during work time. So, over the years, Red Square, the flagpole and the surrounding spaces developed many layers of meaning, and these have to be conveyed in any meaningful interpretation of the site.

Moves towards a rail heritage centre

Late in 2002, the MRA committed to funding a concept planning and business feasibility study for a proposed state rail heritage centre. The MRA invited interested parties onto a steering committee to put together a tender brief. Those invited were the City of Swan, the Swan Chamber of Commerce, the WA Tourism Commission, the Western Australian Railway Historical Society (subsequently Rail Heritage

WA), the Heritage Council of WA, the WA Museum, the Labour History Society and the Workshops History Project. Apart from input in these discussions, it is evident that McCracken's discussion paper influenced the project brief, which stated that: 'The MRA vision for the site is to create a distinctive place where educational, cultural and rail heritage facilities and activities coexist and overlap in a unique way that recalls the past and looks to the future'. This statement indicated considerable progress since the initial *Draft Concept Plan* published by the MRA in August 2000, in which Blocks 1, 2 and 3 were designated for redevelopment as residential or residential over retail, and the closest commitment to a rail heritage centre was the somewhat qualified statement: 'While previous studies show a working rail museum across most of the site is not likely to be commercially viable, the MRA will investigate the feasibility and viability of an active rail museum, limited to Block 1 and retention of active lines to that building'. It would have been unwise, though, for the project members to relax their vigilance. Pressure continued from other bodies such as the Swan Chamber of Commerce, whose plans for the site contained little heritage content and certainly did not include a rail heritage centre.

The outcome of the tendering process was David Farr and Associates' feasibility study, which included a market analysis, an investigation of commercial opportunities and a business feasibility assessment. While Farr recommended devoting large sections of Blocks 1, 2 and 3 to a rail heritage centre, at an estimated cost of $24 million, the study did not identify sources of potential funding. As an interim response, the MRA opened and funded an interpretive centre in the timekeeper's office in April 2005. A 2006 report by Sanmor Consulting disagreed with Farr's recommendation and advocated a quite different approach, which, although still referring to a 'site museum interpretive experience', was much less ambitious. A third report by Forrest and Spiers in 2008 returned to the concept of a rail heritage centre occupying some portion of Block 1. None of the recommendations were acted upon in the ensuing decade. Although the MetRA released a heritage strategy document in 2017, which contained suggestions for how the site could be interpreted, thus far this has been limited to the positioning of some interpretive signage.

The Rail Heritage Interpretive Centre, which opened in the refurbished timekeeper's office at the site's main gate in 2005, contained displays, ephemera and electronic media provided by the History Project, and was used to educate the general public and school parties about the people, the skills and the products of the Midland Government Railway Workshops. The centre was staffed by a part-time coordinator, paid by the MRA, and volunteer guides, whose duties included conducting tours of portions of the site. That said, the interpretive centre was intended to be only a temporary repository for a small portion of the collection. The planned rail heritage centre would serve as a purpose-built repository within one of the heritage-listed buildings, for union and private collections of papers and ephemera, initially gathered by the History Project, but which could have a provenance broader than the Workshops site. Thus, it was envisaged, Midland would be home to a significant collection of material related to the state's (or even Australia's) rail history. While some may regard such a plan as unfeasible, even presumptuous, it is worth noting that the Heritage Council of WA regarded the site as 'the most significant example of an early twentieth century railway Workshop *in Australia*' (my emphasis) and related the Midland Railway Workshops' significance to their intact state and their role in the development of the state's transport networks and industry.

The envisaged repository would also devote exhibition space to objects such as foreigners. Displayed *in situ*, the workers' creative artefacts would have had greater significance and relevance than if removed to another context. The value of context was amply demonstrated in one of the most successful exhibitions staged on site at the 2004 Open Day. *Under the Lap, Over the Fence* displayed 201 foreigner products. Not only had the History Project collected legal items, including a typewriter, a union ballot box, sporting shields, models of engines and of the Workshops site as well as the abovementioned foreigners, but also the Workshops' huge, beautifully crafted boards of honour, which contained the names of employees who served in the world wars, a room full of photographs, a large model of the Workshops layout and many other objects. At the time of this exhibition, the honour boards were still awaiting restoration and adequate display.

Regrettably, after only three years of operation, the Interpretive Centre closed in 2008. Site works to remove pollution had forced the cancellation of the popular heritage tours, the reduction of the hours that the centre was open and eventually brought about its closure. Despite initial promises and the recommendations of the two previously mentioned reports – Farr (2003), Forrest and Spiers (2008) – the centre was not reopened and no museum has taken its place. In 2009, the MRA's website still maintained that

> The Railway Workshops buildings will be adapted for residential and commercial uses, *with Block 1 housing the proposed rail heritage centre.* The Power House, Copper Shop and Pattern Shop will have heritage activities of interest to visitors and may include creative industries and educational opportunities. A walk trail links buildings, equipment and sites, interpreting the former use of the area and recognising the heritage value of the Workshops (my emphasis).

In 2018, there was no mention of a rail heritage centre or a museum anywhere on the MetRA's website, although the *Midland Heritage Interpretation Strategy* (2017) included an appendix devoted to interpreting the main buildings of the Workshops site, with the exception of Block 1, which has been partially converted into a medical centre. This building is still the most appropriate site for a Rail Heritage Centre because the railway lines and inspection pits remain in three-quarters of the building.

To succeed, any proposal requires a working partnership between government and private enterprise, and a capacity to generate income as well as spend it. It was here that the proposal of a rail heritage centre on the Midland Workshops site was most vulnerable. Opportunities existed for generating funds from, for example, the sale of building blocks at the western end, but the vision and the will were lacking. Rail Heritage WA required a site with the space to restore locomotives, rolling stock and fittings, and to operate steam trains for tourists. The Machinery Preservation Society (a long-term occupier of buildings onsite) needed space to demonstrate machinery in operation as well as static displays. These and other organisations had the capacity to train apprentices in the skills required for restoration, including copper smithing, moulding, upholstering, blacksmithing, carpentry, moulding, and fitting and turning. Yet the MRA and its successor, the MetRA, looked elsewhere for tenants for the buildings.

The foundry and the main blocks still contain some machines *in situ*, but not all of the skills practised on site required large spaces, and not all produced large objects. New artisan skills were introduced to the site in the form of light industries in the foundry building, including glass blowers, sculptors and fine wood craftspeople. Craft training, albeit in different skills from those learnt in heavy industry, coincided with the desire expressed by unionists that the site be used again for industry and skills training. There were precedents. At the Ipswich Railway Workshops in 2003, about eighty former railways employees were occupied in traditional skills, such as boilermaking, and fitting and turning, alongside the new railway museum. The Swindon STEAM Museum also contained a workshop a visitors' viewing platform overlooked. I visited the STEAM Museum in 2003 and found its displays to be closer to the History Project's vision for Midland than any other railway museum, including the National Railway Museum at York. The displays attempted to create the sights and sounds of the worksite. As STEAM's web page states:

> Visitors will get a sense of the heat and grime experienced in the Foundry. Then, passing through the Carriage Body Shop ... the sights and sounds of the Machine Shop are evoked. Lathes, drills and slotters were used to manufacture parts to the highest standards. Visitors complete this part of their journey in the Boiler Shop – where the noise endured by the workers meant that many were deaf by the age of 30 – and the Erecting Shop.

The museum was refurbished with the assistance of English Heritage and the Swindon Borough Council's heritage advisor, to ensure the retention of as much as possible of the original fabric of the buildings.

At Midland, too, there was the option of establishing partnerships between private industry, the local city council, heritage groups such as the Rail Heritage WA and the Machinery Preservation Society, and educational institutions to develop training programs in the classic railway trades, although the call for these would always be limited. Midland has the facilities to re-establish a workshop for the rebuilding of steam locomotives and accompanying rolling stock. Oliver and Reeves suggested that Midland could become

> the national rail and tramway restoration workshops, a centre of excellence, undertaking work at Midland or *in situ* for the myriad rail and tram societies [around Australia] that are now seeking to restore or refurbish engines and rolling stock for the community, tourist and heritage railways.

This work could complement training programs. The pattern shop, for example, still contains hundreds of patterns for locomotive parts, and the site retains some of the largest cranes in the state. But the MetRA's vision for Midland is not as an industrial centre, or even, it would appear, as a place that celebrates its industrial past. In 2018 the possibility of establishing a heritage centre seemed more remote than it was in 2005, because Rail Heritage WA, which aimed to maintain and operate historic locomotives and rolling stock out of Block 1, was obliged to vacate the premises. The Interpretive Centre was closed, and all attempts to re-open it had been rebuffed. Despite maintaining the old MRA logo 'Proud history, exciting history', it is clear that the MetRA's vision for Midland is focused more on making future profits than on interpreting the past.

In its heyday the Midland Workshops was the state's largest employer; reputedly, almost everyone in Perth either worked there, or was related to or knew someone who worked there. The workforce included local councillors and future members of the state government. The Workshops' social, economic and political impact upon Western Australia was rightly acknowledged with the 2004 establishment of the site as a heritage icon. Beyond this, the Workshops played a role in Australia's national rail network. Internationally, as part of the British Empire's industrial system, it was a destination for skilled British migrants until the 1970s. Despite its relatively small size, Midland – as the state's only railway workshops – should rank in importance alongside Swindon and Crewe as a major industrial workplace and training site.

Railway workshops, and the rail networks they served, are as much a part of the former British Empire's collective heritage as are European cathedrals; to many people they would be imbued with far more meaning and significance. Yet, so few of these workshops have been retained and interpreted in any meaningful way. In Australia, while Ipswich and Launceston have successful rail museums in operation, this has not happened at Eveleigh, but Eveleigh at least still houses the famous steam locomotive 3801, and other parts of the site retain the original buildings as venues for exhibitions, dramatic arts and markets. At Midland, a major difficulty in establishing a rail heritage centre has been the inability or reluctance of those charged with the feasibility studies to provide realistic guidelines or imaginative suggestions for funding such an enterprise. It is to be hoped that the time for establishing a rail heritage centre at Midland is not yet past. If it has, we shall all be the poorer.

2
Interpreting Workers' Space

This chapter discusses the challenges we faced when we attempted to represent workers' space in a proposed industrial heritage centre on the WAGR Workshops site. I will demonstrate how the principles that undergirded the History Project on the site complemented recommendations by other heritage practitioners. Preliminary discussions strongly endorsed the need for a centre to reflect the uniqueness of Midland, not one that merely copied overseas or interstate museums.

The vision

Today, the Workshops site is managed by MetRA, an amalgamation of several urban redevelopment authorities. During the life of the Workshops History Project, Midland had its own separate Midland Redevelopment Authority (MRA), a government authority that had a fifteen year tenure in which to redevelop the area now named Helena Precinct because of its proximity to the Helena River. The main buildings on the site were assessed by the Heritage Council of WA as having significant heritage value. During 2004, the 175th anniversary of European settlement in Western Australia, members of the public were asked to nominate 'heritage icons' from the natural or built environment, phenomena, ceremonies, inventions or objects. The Workshops was one of thirteen such items granted heritage icon status.

But what, if anything, did this actually mean for the development of a heritage centre on the site? Australia has had many industrial sites with fine buildings that have not been preserved. Comparison has been

Curtin student Susan Hall and Project Coordinator Ric McCracken with one of the exhibits in the Workshops Closure exhibition in 2004. (Photo courtesy of Bobbie Oliver)

made between such institutions the Altoona Railroaders Memorial Museum and the STEAM Museum at Swindon. At Midland, the workers' contribution was recognised in the construction of the Workers Wall. But more was needed.

The *Heritage Strategy* (2002) stated that all site features of 'exceptional significance and considerable significance' should be 'retained and preserved', and that areas of 'exceptional or considerable significance' should be 'retained as open space'. Honouring these specifications required sensitive re-interpretation of the redeveloped site, so that it would still be possible to recognise the former use of the buildings, and the streetscape should not be significantly altered. Beyond that, the streetscape should retain an authentic industrial feel. Could this requirement be satisfied by giving additions to the site, such as roads, names that related to the Workshops' past? Presently, these include Railway Square for the large open space west of the main blocks, Foundry Road, which runs across the site and into the housing development on the eastern shore of the Coal Dam (which fortunately has retained its original designation, rather than being changed to 'lake'), Woodmill Lane, Crucible Lane and Furnace Road. Most of these names are quite generic and could relate to any major industrial site; only Turntable Walk and Railway Square bear specific reference to their railway heritage. Conversely, the streets around the Coal Dam have been given the names of coal companies that operated in Collie, the source of most of the coal used in the steam era: Wallsend, Wyvern, Centaur, Griffin, Stockton and Cardiff.

While it is satisfying to see that an attempt was made to maintain a historical link with the Coal Dam's history, it begs the question as to why this degree of specificity could not have been observed throughout the site. The only person associated with the Workshops who has been commemorated on the site by name is Charles Yelverton O'Connor (Yelverton Drive, formerly Montreal Road East). The Workshops' connection with O'Connor is not as strong as is often supposed. Although he recommended the site and submitted a design for the Workshops, he resigned from his position as acting general manager of the WAGR seven years before the initial buildings were completed. His design was not used, the basis of the layout that exists today being designed by the completely unsung Thomas Rotherham. Apart from Yelverton Drive, there is nothing among the site names given to roads and lanes that is specific to the Midland Government Railway Workshops. Not even the names of CMEs are used, much less those of union officials or other workers.

Adopting historical names is one of the easier ways of acknowledging the past. Preserving the site's stories *in situ* is a far more complex matter. How might these stories be preserved in the public domain so that they remain evident in the fabric and purposes of the site? The Workshops was designed to build and repair steam locomotives from the commencement of their construction, through to the various stages to the completion of a new engine, or from the time a locomotive entered for repair, through to the stripping down and the replacement of parts, to the end of the line where it emerged as a repaired engine. How might the story of that process be preserved if the various elements, such as machinery, the rails upon which the engines and parts were moved or inspection pits over which they stood are taken up or filled in? Some items, such as the mighty drop hammer in Block 2, would be difficult to move, but other more portable elements have gone.

The evidence of social interaction is even more ephemeral. Now that the lathes have been removed from Block 3, there is nothing to mark where Red Square is. It is just part of a large, bare floor. How can the story of this spirited subversion of authority be demonstrated? In some places on the site, interpretation panels have been created to assist visitors to understand what was once there. Presently, Block 3 is off limits to the public, so how and where can the story of Red Square be told?

From the workers' viewpoint, one of the most important activities at the Workshops was the flagpole meetings. Indeed, to them, the flagpole was *the* focal point of the Workshops. An interpretive panel by the flagpole explains the site's significance, but this could have been emphasised by adopting a name for the square that is more empathetic, a name that might raise visitors' curiosity, such as Flagpole Meeting Square or Union Square.

It is also ironic that the name Railway Square has been adopted for a space that used to be crossed with numerous railway tracks running to each of the main blocks, and yet today have all been removed except for those that enter Block 1. To what extent are the railway lines integral to the streetscape of the square? History Project members believed that they were, and that they should not have been removed. Interpretive panels are a step in the right direction, but they are an inadequate substitute for a genuine site interpretation. This involves conveying essential aspects to achieve an accurate historical interpretation of an industrial site, and to engage the interest and understanding of future generations of visitors. What follows are some examples of those essential aspects.

First, there was the atmosphere of the place, which can be retrieved only through interviews with former workers and contemporary film of the Workshops in action. It was a hot (or cold, depending on the season), uncomfortable, noisy and dangerous place to work. Interviewees described the Workshops as being 'like Dante's inferno', 'hot', 'smoky' and 'full of dust', a place where minor injuries caused by metal or wood splinters occurred daily, and noise levels were so great they gave workers tinnitus or permanent deafness.

Part of this atmosphere (or ethos) is the mythology. According to official records, there were twenty-two fatalities between 1903 and 1973. As yet no comparative study has been undertaken to ascertain how this fatality rate compares with similar factories for the era, but it would appear to be fairly low, considering the hazards of the workplace and the lack of safety equipment. Problems arise as the records do not always concur with the recollections of past employees. Neil McDougall, a fitter who began his training in 1961, could 'remember several men being killed in there'. In particular he remembered an accident, also recalled by several other workers, in which 'something went wrong' with the slotting machine in the machine shop. The operator 'put his head under the slotter' to ascertain why it had stopped. It came down suddenly and 'smashed his head like a walnut'. McDougall also mentioned that one of his apprentices, an apprentice fitter, fell 'off the side of a locomotive, and, well, he didn't come back to work. He died that night.' The records show that the only fatality recorded in the 1960s did indeed involve a shunting locomotive, but the employee was listed as being G. A. Kenworthy, a car builder, not a fitter, whereas the slotting machine accident that killed apprentice B. Humphrey occurred on 25 March 1957, while McDougall was still at school.

Another accident that was vivid in the collective memory occurred even earlier in the foundry, when a blockage in the cupola caused hot metal to build up. When it was cleared, by the usual method of poking with a long rod, the molten metal spewed out of the bottom of the cupola and across the floor where men were working. Moulder's assistant A. H. Green died of burns some days afterwards. Several other workers were seriously injured. Although this accident occurred in 1943, it was often referred to by workers of a later era as having occurred 'just before my time'. Perhaps this was because the horror of the accident was so deeply etched that workers owned the event, continually referring to it almost as if they had been eye witnesses.

It is difficult to convey to modern audiences the scant regard for safety in industrial workplaces in the mid and even later twentieth century. Safety remains an issue on industrial worksites, even in the twenty-first century era of hard hats and high-viz vests. Before legislation enforced the use of safety equipment in 1984, many workers eschewed even basic gear such as safety goggles and ear protectors. Old boilermakers would joke about their industrial deafness. Others have paid and continue to pay the even higher price of working among the deadly asbestos fibres from fire retardant lagging that was wrapped around locomotive boilers. Photographs prior to the 1980s show workers in ordinary shirts, trousers and felt hats working with molten metal. Foundry workers were equipped with leather gloves and long leather aprons, but they were the exception to most. Even with the help of contemporary images, it is difficult, almost impossible, to convey fully what the place was like, partly because video and audio recordings do not reproduce the type and especially the level of noise that workers endured on a daily basis, although some have done a competent job of describing it. A comparison familiar to some would be to compare the noise of a steam locomotive on film to the noise made by a real engine. The noise levels of an industrial workplace have to be experienced to be fully appreciated. Peter Carty, who was interviewed on film for the Workshops History Project, stated that his wife and a neighbour once came on a visit to the shop floor. He said that they were 'open mouthed' with astonishment at the level of noise.

Second, there are the traditions. Every factory has its initiations, but the Peanut King, an elaborate initiation ceremony that was practised all over the Workshops with variations from one shop to another, may have been unique to Midland (see chapter 4). How can historians and heritage practitioners interpret ceremonies such as the Peanut King? We are fortunate to have photographs and recorded descriptions by onlookers and participants in the Peanut King, but each experience affected an individual in a unique way. In many cases, we do not know how prank victims felt.

The Workshops' closure

My third example of challenges in interpretation concerns the Workshops' closure. On the day in April 1993 when the workers were summoned to a meeting where they would learn that the Workshops was going to be closed, the television cameras recorded footage of their faces as they received the news. The initial shock felt by workers is clear from the video images, but it is from the interviews collected by the Workshops History Project that we realised, even years after the event, memories were still raw. Looking at the shock and despair on the men's faces recorded on the television news footage inspired me to write chapter 7, in which I urge employers and policy makers to consider the human cost of site closures and redundancies.

The Workshops History Project demonstrated that the stories we tell and the interpretations we make are often divisive. Nowhere is this more evident than in narratives surrounding the closure of the Workshops. The soft option is to tell it as a story of inevitability, that by the 1990s the age of large industrial workshops had gone, that the Workshops was uncompetitive with private enterprise, and was incurring substantial annual losses, so it was evitable – and a sign of 'progress' – that the factory would close. It was just a matter of when. That was the preferred version adopted by the MRA. For historians, the issues were far more complex. We have to be careful to ensure we are not dealing out sanitised history that tells only part of the story.

Another narrative was that it was really the trade unions' fault because they had become too demanding, and so priced the Workshops out of the market. Because of their demands the place was just not competitive in an age of economic rationalism. This story offended the very people who wanted the workers' stories told in the first place, and while it contained some elements of truth, was it any more accurate than the first one? Yet another interpretation was the one that appealed to the unions: the Workshops was an efficient and competent outfit that was closed down as a deliberate strategy of a union-smashing state government. Again, there were elements of truth but it was not the whole story.

This is a story that features prominently in the recollections of former Workshops employees. The ulterior motives of the government and private industry form a recurring theme in these interviews. Patrick Gayton, for example, a pattern maker, who was not particularly pro-union, stated that his reaction to the Workshops closure was anger. 'I still am [angry] because I've been a worker all my life. It provided work, it put food on the table. It provided apprenticeships for the youngsters … [I was] particularly [angry] with [Premier] Court.' Peter Carty, a boilermaker, who was diagnosed with asbestosis during the life of the History Project, put it more strongly when he claimed: 'The government used the thing against us – and the Chamber of Commerce [too] – that the government work can't compete against private industry because they're taking private industry work away; that's the sort of thing that was fronted up to us.' The interviews expressing these sentiments were conducted a decade after the closure was announced, yet it is clear that both of these men still felt strong emotions about the circumstances.

Telling the workers' stories

The history the project collected had elements of all of these accounts, but, more importantly, it revealed individual stories of the redundancies, at least one suicide, the depression and the impact on Midland, always a struggling, working class town. Peter Carty's comments graphically represent the anguish reflected by so many workers:

> They sacked all these bloody people ... they [didn't] debrief you. If you've been trained up to that and you're good at what you're doing [and] they don't debrief you, meaning that, okay, this is going to happen and that's going happen. All those clever bastards, you know. How do you tell thousands of blokes that? They just shut the gate.

The stories were told in various ways apart from the written word. Here is one example of how the History Project intervened to tell history 'as it happened'. In 2004, the MRA celebrated the centenary of the Workshops opening in 1904, but they were strangely reluctant to commemorate the decade of the closure. The History Project decided to stage an exhibition on 4 March 2004, the tenth anniversary of the closure. The display, curated by the Project Coordinator, Ric McCracken and Susan Hall, a Curtin University Graduate Diploma student, included a table and chairs where people could sit and chat or look at the various objects, and a book where they could write their reactions to the exhibition and to the closure. Five hundred people passed through the exhibition in the three days that it was open, and many of the comments reflected the residual bitterness that many still felt about the Workshops closing.

Exhibitions are one way of interpreting a site's experiences; another is in the design of refurbished buildings. Although the Interpretive Centre has been closed for over a decade, on the blinds, visible from outside of the building, one can still see the photographic images of the workers entering and leaving the Workshops at the beginning and end of the day. The Interpretive Centre was located in the timekeeper's office just inside the main gate, where the workers collected or deposited their metal identity discs at the beginning and end of each day. The design on the blinds was one way of conveying the size of a workforce of 2000–3000 people, and the life and movement associated with a large industrial worksite. Now that the site is silent and in limbo, this image conveys the pathos of an active, industrial past that becomes even more remote with the continuing offshore location of major Australian industries.

What then is the significance of studying the lives of these people? Does it matter if, a generation hence, while the products made by their hands remain, the stories of their lives are lost? Labour historians believe that it matters a great deal. When we lose these stories, we lose part of the history of our society and our understanding of the past. Beyond helping us to explore the experience of working in a large industrial workplace in Midland, knowledge of these lives – their skills, their work practices, their customs, their working conditions – enables us to make contrasts and comparisons with workers elsewhere. The closure of railway workshops and rail infrastructure occurred all over the former British Empire from the 1960s onwards. In Britain, many lives were profoundly affected by the closure of one-third of all railway lines and by major railway workshops, such as Swindon, ceasing operations. These closures became known as the Beeching Axe, after Richard Beeching, then chairman of British Rail, who recommended the cuts. Australia and New Zealand experienced similar closures in the 1980s and 1990s.

One could read between the lines the bitterness of the anonymous author of a website devoted to the Addington Railway Workshops at Christchurch, New Zealand (closed in December 1990 and since demolished), when he wrote that the Workshops was 'torn down because of the prevailing New Right doctrine at the time'. The website also disappeared several years ago. Bitterness and bewilderment were clearly reflected on the faces of the men at Midland, who television film crews recorded in 1993, after they received news that the Workshops would close the following year. Lives separated by thousands of kilometres were bound by the common inheritance of working in the railways. Just how much is similar and how much is unique to each worksite is yet to be ascertained, for there is so much still to learn. Making the knowledge accessible to scholars and the interested public is part of that challenge. If the research already done is not being made available in the public sphere, there is far less chance of further enquiry being undertaken.

Of course, the products of the Workshops History Project, whether archival material or published research, could be displayed anywhere, but, as I have indicated, displays *in situ* have an immediacy and create an interest that might otherwise be lacking. There are many arguments for interpreting the Workshops site in a comprehensible way. The following chapters discuss the heritage significance of the WAGR Workshops as a site of the British Empire diaspora of skilled workers, initiation ceremonies among apprentices, the political battleground of the Cold War, the transformation of technology in the twentieth century, and the ramifications of privatisation.

3
Midland Workshops as a Site of the British Diaspora

The WAGR Midland Workshops site is historically significant for many reasons, and not just for the state of Western Australia, but also for Australia as a whole and even other parts of the former British empire. This chapter will employ the concept of diaspora to refer to British skilled labour, ideas and technology that were spread around the empire during the nineteenth century. As a result of a physical and cultural diaspora from Britain, Australia was constructed as a British nation in the Asian region. Subsequently, elements of Britishness, introduced at different points in post-settlement Australian history, constitute what might be termed a cultural diaspora. Among these British elements, industrial complexes have left a clearly distinguishable imprint upon the landscape. The form of diaspora being examined here is that of the nineteenth century railway workshop, with specific reference to the WAGR Workshops at Midland.

Railway workshops constructed in Glasgow, Crewe or Swindon (1840s), Christchurch or Dunedin in New Zealand in the 1870s and 1880s, or any of the major railway workshops constructed around Australia, such as Ipswich (1860s), Eveleigh (1880s) or Midland (1910s), were built as if to a blueprint. On these sites, there arose the physical geography of saw-toothed roofs – cleverly designed to maximise available light in an age before electricity – that surmounted long, wide buildings divided into bays for tools and machinery. It is easy to imagine that, because of the geographical similarity of the layout and the fact that British engines and rolling stock were used, a worker could have travelled around the British empire and felt relatively at home in any railway workshop, whether in Australia, South Africa, India or New Zealand.

Indeed, a past employee of the Midland Railway Workshops, who had completed his apprenticeship in the latter part of the twentieth century, on seeing a photograph of the Swindon Workshops (c. 1915) remarked, 'That's just like Midland'. Likewise, the skilled British tradesman would have had little difficulty in fitting into the system of industrial labour organisation in any of these overseas locations.

The British origin of Australian skilled trades and trade unionism

According to British labour historian Eric Hobsbawm, the numbers of trade unions and trade unionists expanded massively during the 1880s and 1890s. He wrote that several factors initiated this expansion, including unionism within the transport and mining industries and the development of new types of unions (the general and the industrial). This widened 'the field of union organisation and action, of strategy

A comparison between the No. 3 Erecting Shop at Crewe in 1903 (above) and the Erecting Shop at Midland, c. 1910 (opp.), shows the similarity in design of railway workshops across the British Empire. (1903 photo: courtesy of Railway Museum UK; 1910 photo: courtesy of the Midland Railway Workshops History collection)

and tactics, and inter-union coordination'. Strategies adopted by union leaders included national strikes and lockouts and 'a sharp turn to the left' in ideology. Another factor was the formation of unions of unskilled workers, which historians have termed 'new unionism'. Comparative studies have shown that new unionism, characterised by the organisation of unskilled, politically militant workers, developed concurrently in other countries, but that, in Europe, the British movement was unique in one feature – the pre-existence of a well-established base of old trade unionism, consisting of conservative and elite groups of skilled craftsmen. In the eastern states of Australia – or colonies as they were prior to 1901 – a similar development occurred.

While the development of British and Australian trade unions occurred simultaneously from the 1850s, undoubtedly the most powerful influence on colonial Australian trade unions in the nineteenth and early twentieth centuries came from Britain, in the form of personnel and ideas. Tom Mann, a leader of the 1889 London dock strike, for example, spent several years in Australia, while visiting labour men included Ben Tillett and Kier Hardie. Many union leaders, including Mann, Tom Walsh and W. P. Earsman were British-born and, in some cases, were seasoned unionists by the time they arrived in Australia.

Many of the trades developed in the factories of the British industrial era. The stonemasons' and coach builders' societies were much older, but likewise originated in Britain. The craftsmen, such as cabinet and coach makers, jealously guarded their elite status, ensuring that only fully skilled workers could enter their membership. Craft unions preferred more moderate forms of protest, such as petitions to their employers, generally eschewing the more militant methods favoured particularly by miners and textile workers, such as the strike. Australian unions also held to this distinction until the major defeats of the 1890s forced them to consider political power, and then arbitration, as alternatives.

Craft unions had been active in the Australian colonies since the 1830s and made early gains, such as the eight hour working day, which was achieved in 1856 by the Melbourne Stonemasons Union, and a six and a half day week gained in the 1870s. Australian skilled trade unions closely paralleled the British craft unions, although they were usually separate unions. The Amalgamated Engineering Union (AEU), which formed in Sydney in 1852, was a branch of the British union, with which it maintained a relationship until 1968. The AEU's historian, Tom Sheridan, wrote that the union maintained its elite status by limiting entry to men between the ages of 21 and 40 years, who had undergone at least five years training at their trade. Similarly, historian Ian Turner observed that, like their British counterparts, Australian craft unions protected their interests by 'restricting entry through the apprenticeship system, by establishing wages and conditions of work appropriate to the craftsman's dignity, and by providing financial help in case of unemployment, sickness or death'.

Craft union members tended to be politically moderate or conservative, although the AEU was an exception. Another union, the Australian Society of Engineers (ASE), which covered the same trades, was moderate. Both of these unions operated at the Midland Railway Workshops, as did unions of semiskilled or unskilled workers, such as the Australian Workers' Union (AWU), and the Western Australian Amalgamated Society of Railway Employees (WAASRE), which represented a broad range of railway workers, with the exception of footplate staff, who were covered by the Locomotive Engine Drivers', Firemen's and Cleaners' Union (LED).

In most states, as in Britain, unions were affiliated with independent trades and labor councils (TLCs). While the Trades Union Congress (TUC), the peak body in Britain, had been formed in 1868, Australia's peak union body, the Australian Council of Trades Unions (ACTU), came on the scene relatively late in 1928. State TLCs became the ACTU's representative in most states, except in Western Australia, which did not establish an independent TLC until 1963.

Another Western Australian distinction was that, prior to the era of new unionism, there was very little trade union activity of any type. The WA labour movement developed amid very different circumstances from those in the eastern colonies. Upon its foundation in 1829, the colony had inherited legislation enacted during the reign of George IV, including the 1825 Conspiracy Law, and laws conferring illegality on all trade union activity, to which the colonial government added other oppressive laws that remained in force until the twentieth century. Under the *Master and Servant Act* (1842), servants could be jailed for up to six months for failing to properly perform their duties. Convict transportation to Western Australia commenced in 1842 and continued until 1868, long after its cessation elsewhere. Yet despite being denied legal status, the unions that formed in the 1880s and 1890s were not suppressed. Early craft unions included the Amalgamated Society of Carpenters and Joiners, formed 1884, the first Locomotive Engine Drivers' and Firemen's Union (1885), and the Typographical Society (1889). The Fremantle Lumpers Union (FLU), the colony's predecessor to the Waterside Workers Federation (WWF) and the first major union of unskilled workers in Western Australia, was founded in 1889. Five craft unions formed a Trades and Labor Council in Perth in 1891, but coastal labour solidarity was severely weakened by strong parochial rivalries between Perth and Fremantle, and a conservative prejudice against dabbling in politics. Fremantle's enmity towards Perth increased when the railway workshops was relocated from there to Midland Junction in 1904. In this vast, rural state, the WAGR Workshops became the state's most significant industrial workforce. It operated as a closed shop – another tradition brought from Britain.

The British industrial diaspora's impact on trade unions

Despite these national and local distinctions, the trade union system in Australia still closely resembled that in Britain. This resulted from the diaspora of British tradesmen, at least some of whom came to Australia either because they were frustrated by the timidity of their own union, or after being blacklisted in Britain because of their involvement in strike action. An example of the former may be found in Robert Hollis, who was born in 1851 in Derbyshire. At 13, he went to work at the Midland Railway Company, reaching the grade of engine driver in 1878 at the age of 27. He was an active member of the Amalgamated Society of Railway Servants, and was elected to its executive, but he was disappointed by the union's conservatism. While other railwaymen sought a solution in forming a sectional union, the Associated Society of Locomotive Engineers and Firemen (ASLEF), in Sheffield in 1880, Hollis instead decided to emigrate. In 1884 he and his wife, Alice, arrived in New South Wales, where Hollis joined the Railway Department and soon became general secretary of the NSW Locomotive Engine Drivers', Firemen's and Cleaners' Association which was founded 1883. Hollis' experiences in England convinced him of the value of a union dedicated to drivers, firemen and cleaners, and he opposed attempts by another English immigrant, William Schey, to organise all railway workers, including stationmasters, guards, porters and signalmen, into one union.

A particularly bitter strike by ASLEF members employed by the Midland Railway Company in Britain in 1887 resulted in some railwaymen being blacklisted and their service records inscribed 'Not to be used in the United Kingdom'. The union, which encouraged them to emigrate, provided grants to assist families to relocate to other countries. How many came to Western Australia is unknown but, in that one year, the ASLEF records showed that fifty-six members took the opportunity to emigrate.

Others, like Hollis, came to Australia to set up unions in an environment that they saw as being less influenced by authoritarian private railway bosses. To some extent, their assumptions were correct, but the colonial governments could be similarly authoritarian. William Somerville, Western Australia's first labour historian, wrote of conditions in the colony in the 1880s and 1890s, that 'There was no union to stand up for the rights of the [railway] worker and no Labour Party to appeal to'. After an earlier attempt failed, the West Australian Locomotive Engine Drivers', Firemen's and Cleaners Union (LED) formed in 1898. Despite this, wrote Somerville, gaining improved working conditions was 'no easy task', as it was unpopular to talk of unionism and unionists were branded as agitators. Even in Victoria, where the railway drivers' union was formed in 1861 – prior to any of the British railway unions – it had to overcome many difficulties, including the fact that the railway commissioners were given complete control over employing, retaining, classifying and promoting staff.

Training and career structures

The British influence showed in the career structure for footplate staff and the training requirements for trades apprentices. Although lacking a specific apprenticeship, the footplate staff usually began as engine cleaners or, even before that, as call boys, and then progressed, between the ages of 18 and 21, to fireman. After several years as fireman, a man could pass an examination to become a driver of shunting engines, and then gradually climb the ranks to being a top ranked passenger express train driver. By 1914 there was an established line of promotion from call boy (or caller up, as they were sometimes called in Britain) to cleaner. A minimum height requirement of 5 feet 6 inches (168 centimetres) was required for footplate staff, but not for Workshops employees. One boy who applied for promotion to cleaner in the WAGR was rejected because he was only 5 feet 3¼ inches (160 centimetres), but he was accepted a for a position in the boiler shop at the Railway Workshops. He may have been too small to clean engines but he wasn't too small to be a boilermaker's apprentice. No doubt, being small had its advantages when the work required crawling into locomotive boilers. The British minimum height requirements were shorter: a British cleaner had to be 5 feet 2 inches at age 14, and 5 foot 4 inches at age 16.

Trades apprenticeships, too, were part of the industrial system that Australia inherited from Britain. From 1901 Australian apprentices' conditions were regulated by either state or commonwealth Acts, under which the minimum age was lifted for most workers from 12 to 14 years and the maximum working week set at 48 hours. All of the skilled tradesmen who were employed at the Workshops had completed a trades apprenticeship; the relevant union insisted upon that requirement being met.

The elitism engendered by lengthy training and graduating to a skilled trade was clearly evident in the reminiscences of Midland Railway Workshops past employees. At the end of the 1930s, Jack Emery's family made sacrifices so that he could train as an apprentice turner and iron machinist, because they strongly believed that 'They can't take a trade off you'. A working class that had suffered bitterly in the economic depression of the 1930s, believed that having a trade offered security and the promise of ongoing employment in hard times when unskilled workers lost their jobs.

In Britain and Australia, tradesmen were regarded as elites, an opinion reinforced by a higher wage than the wage for unskilled workers, and by the exclusion of women from trade training. Some local features helped to enforce this view. The compulsory arbitration system, adopted from New Zealand at the beginning of the twentieth century, instituted in law the conditions and wages of workers and permitted representatives of registered unions and employers' organisations to argue their case before a court president, without legal counsel. The distinctiveness of the Australian system was increased by the 1907 Harvester judgement, which introduced a basic wage, calculated on the living expenses of a married man with two children. This judgement served to gender the wage system, as it assumed that women were not breadwinners; thus, even females with dependents were paid approximately 50 per cent of the male wage, rising to 75 per cent only when women undertook what was deemed to be men's work during World War II. The first equal pay legislation, granting equal pay for equal work was passed in 1969. The basic wage was for unskilled workers; margins were added for skills, thus reinforcing the hierarchy of skilled craftsmen. The workforce was yet more deeply gendered by the division of occupations into male and female. No women were employed as skilled industrial tradespeople in railway workshops until the late 1980s.

The second half of the twentieth century saw massive changes to the trades' apprenticeship system in Australia and Britain, and with these began the erosion of elites. In 1952, the first National Inquiry Into Apprenticeships recommended shortening Australian apprenticeships from five (or in some cases six) years to four years and extending opportunities for off-the-job training courses. Under the standard training methods, which persisted in many workshops until the 1970s, apprentices were expected to learn chiefly by watching their coworker tradesmen, and then doing the task themselves. Changes to the apprenticeship system in Australia, especially from the 1980s, resulted in a wide variety of training schemes being made available to young women, as well as men, in a range of trades and occupations. In 2000, 31 per cent of apprentices were female, compared with 16.5 per cent in 1995. Traditionally, the apprenticeship system was focused exclusively upon trade certificate or equivalent qualifications; today, it has been extended to cover all levels of vocational qualifications. Apprenticeships now range from a few months to more than three years duration, but the majority of trainees prefer the longer apprenticeships. Evidently, the traditional, male-dominated, blue-collar work culture, where status was determined by the practice of a skilled trade, has largely been replaced by a broader, more inclusive and less class-based system of vocational training. These changes form part of the dismantling of the arbitration system that was the hallmark of Australian industrial relations for almost a century. A similar expansion of the apprenticeship system occurred in Britain, especially after New Labour gained government in 1997.

British culture at Midland Railway Workshops

In its role as the foremost trainer of industrial apprentices in Western Australia, the Workshops was the largest of only three or four major factories around Perth where boys learnt a range of trades, such as blacksmithing, boilermaking, fitting, mechanical and electrical engineering, machining, coach building and carpentry – the skills required to build and repair locomotive engines and rolling stock, but that also equipped the men for a wide range of trades outside the railways. The Workshops was a tightly knit community, within which a range of subcommunities, centred on the different trades, thrived in a proud and highly competitive working culture. Much of that culture was derived from British antecedents.

Historian Kathy Bell observed of the Midland Workshops employees that 'a large proportion of the craftsmen [during the interwar period], especially the older men, were immigrants from Britain. This would explain the apparent similarity between the attitudes and customs of the workshops' tradesmen and those of the 'respectable' section of the British working class.' Bell suggested further evidence of British influence in the closed shop that existed at the Workshops and in the dominance of moderate views. The 'Communistic crowd' was a small minority (see chapter 5). Bell's observations about the influence of British immigrants and British customs were confirmed by former employees. Ivan McMillan recalled the foreman of the fitting shop during the time of his apprenticeship.

> He was a stern-faced man with greying hair and he wore the obligatory navy pants and waistcoat, complete with greasy tie. A pocket watch chain across his belly completed the picture. This was the uniform of the traditional British tradesman of the time it seemed, though why one would want to wear a tie in those circumstances was beyond me.

Craft elites in Britain and Australia

Another aspect of the culture was competition among the crafts. Steve Smith, who began as an apprentice boilermaker in 1972, recalled an era when boilermakers were regarded as 'the king', because they built the steam locomotives; the fitters merely fitted the components. The hierarchy shifted with the changes in technology (see chapter 6). In the world of diesel engines, it was fitters who assumed the status of king. Trade elites also were evident in British factories. Alfred Williams, a former hammerman, wrote that at the Swindon Workshops in the early twentieth century, 'the fitters are usually looked upon as the men *par excellence* of the [fitting] shed', partly because of their wide experience in a range of workplaces.

At Midland, the changing technology affected the craft status of boilermakers and blacksmiths in particular. Removal of their craft status was devastating for some workers, but blacksmiths were able to reinvent themselves. The Workshops began replacing old wooden wagons with aluminium ones, so work that had traditionally required carpenters' skills became blacksmiths' work. Dieselisation brought in another change, perhaps subtler but nevertheless very much in the tradesmen's consciousness. Although the Workshops continued to manufacture items ranging from heavy machinery and bridge girders to small precision tools, and undertook repair of diesel locomotives, new diesel engines were imported, not manufactured on site as the steam locomotives had been. Thus a new trades elite arose (see chapter 6). According to Bill Kirkham, the Workshops' last master of apprentices, the most promising applicants were encouraged to take up apprenticeships as electrical fitters.

Technological change at Midland roughly paralleled that in the

"In the British mould". Workshops foremen in the inter-war period. Note that only one (far right, middle row) is not wearing a tie. (Photo courtesy of Charlie Coote)

eastern Australian states and overseas. Lucy Taksa has observed that, from the mid 1950s, 'technological change associated with dieselisation' at Eveleigh Workshops 'led to a gradual decline in Eveleigh's workforce, so that only 300 remained by the time the shops were closed in 1989'. According to records, Midland staff numbers (excluding apprentices) appear to have peaked at 2850 in 1956, with the highest number of apprentices (557) being registered in 1957. Addington Railway Workshops at Christchurch was constructing its own diesel engines during the 1960s, having built twenty-six shunter DSC class engines between 1962 and 1967. Like Midland, staff numbers at Addington were severely reduced during the 1980s, and the Workshops closed in 1991. While much of the trauma of downsizing occurred in Australia and New Zealand after dieselisation, in Britain, the introduction of diesel engines in the mid to late 1950s was soon overshadowed by the 1963 Beeching recommendation to close as many as one-third of all British railway lines. An underlying factor of these reductions is that governments in each country – whatever their political persuasion – saw road transport as the way of the future. The impact of this transformation at Midland is explored further in Chapter 7. In Western Australia, non-Labor governments in particular pursued a policy of closing railway lines, including suburban commuter routes, but this policy was not to be the downfall of the Midland Railway Workshops; rather, it was the preference for privatisation, embraced by both sides of politics in the 1980s and 1990s.

This chapter has endeavoured to show the significance of the Midland Railway Workshops as a site of industrial diaspora within the British empire. The Workshops' workforce exemplified one particular aspect of Britishness – the system of industrial trades – which was contested by and incorporated into community and self-identities within Australia. I have suggested that the Workshops site has a significance beyond Australia in representing the British industrial diaspora that occurred across the empire in the nineteenth and early twentieth centuries.

To this Britishness can be added local innovations, such as arbitration and particular customs (see chapter 4), in shaping the Workshops' culture and technology. While many developments – especially union-won reforms such as the eight-hour day – occurred contemporaneously with, or even ahead of, similar developments in Britain, others, including the conciliation and arbitration system, were adopted to a much fuller extent in Australia and New Zealand than they were in Britain. Despite these differences, a comparison of railway workshops in Britain, New Zealand and the eastern and western states of Australia suggests that there are enough similarities in origin, work culture, physical structures and industrial organisation (including trade types and skills, apprenticeship training, unions and the closed shop system) to indicate the dispersion of a culture that had a common place or beginning – that is, a diaspora of British industrial culture.

4
Midland Railway Workshops: A site of initiation

Another aspect of Workshops life that reflected the influence of the British diaspora was the practice of initiation ceremonies, which apprentices and sometimes tradesmen inflicted upon new boys. Generations of apprentices had been subjected to pranks and initiations, which were often humiliating but seldom life threatening. During the 1970s and 1980s, these pranks assumed a darker nature. There were incidents of apprentices being suspended from a crane in a cruciform position and pelted with rubbish, threatened with rape, and having their genitals smeared with fibre glass resin or graphite grease, which caused severe burns. This aspect of Workshops life presents many difficulties for interpreters, some of which will be addressed later in the chapter.

The rituals were grounded in British industrial tradition. Former hammer man Alfred Williams described similar experiences endured by apprentices at Swindon in the early years of the twentieth century, although it was sometimes psychological, rather than physical, cruelty.

> The boys were always frightened at the thought of one painful ordeal which they were told they would have to undergo. They were seriously informed by their new mates in the shed that they would have to be branded on the back parts with a hot iron stamp containing the initials of the railway company [GWR], and very many youngsters firmly believed the tale and awaited the operation with dreadful suspense. As time went on, however, and they were not sent for to the offices, they came to discredit the story and smiled at their former credulity.

Williams also mentioned pranks very similar to those experienced at Midland, whereby unsuspecting apprentices were sent to the engine house for a bucket of blast (a telling off) or a toe punch (a kick in the backside).

Steve Smith, a boilermaker who worked at Midland with old tradesmen who had done their training in the steam era and new tradesmen who were trained in the diesel era, imputed the rise in violence largely to the frustrations brought about by changing circumstances: the move from an old craft-based system in which value was placed on the skill of an individual, to a mass-produced product created under assembly line conditions. Consequently, Smith believed, the younger tradesmen lost their respect for the craft and adopted a careless attitude to their work. The discipline on the shop floor declined and this was reflected in initiations 'getting out of control'. Smith described a range of experiences that he endured as an apprentice.

> One of the ... standard tricks – yeah, I nearly died when it happened to me. Get an arc welder; one tradesman would hold the earth, and the other would hold the hand piece with the bare electrode. Now when you touched each other ... you made an electrical circuit. You wait until a young apprentice is walking down the middle of the shop floor and you would both walk up to him [and say] 'How are you?' and you would both touch him on the side of the neck at the same time. When it happened to me, of course, I went flat on my back on the floor. You just received an electric shock you weren't ready for ....

> [At] Christmas time ... we used to have initiations between blacksmiths and the boilermakers. One year I was working [with] my old tradesman Norm Golding. The blacksmiths had thrown a bucket or water over him, so he picked up a big rivet gun, pointed the rivet gun which has got a steel snap that's about [an] inch and [a] half diameter, two inches long – it's like a shotgun – and started shooting at the blacksmiths.

> We had the old troughs in those days where you had ... big steel brackets at the sides, and they grabbed me and threw me into the trough and I ... cracked three ribs on the left-hand side and of course all of a sudden you're down and ... it's like, 'Oh, we're sorry. Don't say anything. Quick, take him to the ambulance section. Oh, he fell over on the job....' [On another occasion] I had my foot broken ... [Then there were] the horrible initiations ...[in] the pits out the back of the diesel shop ... full of horrible oily rubbish. They would throw the apprentices in there to initiate them.

> There was some serious injuries [with] kids because there was steel and everything in the bottom. Kids getting thrown in there and getting speared, breaking limbs and those sort of things ...

While some of the tradesmen who were interviewed for the History Project didn't let the truth get in the way of a good story, these recollections describe situations that are all potentially lethal. There were some instances where interviewees claimed that an apprentice died as a result of an initiation ceremony, even as late as the 1970s, although the records don't support this. According to records kept by the WAGR (or Westrail as it became in 1975), the last fatality at the Workshops occurred in 1967 and it was not of an apprentice. While Smith's recollections of initiation ceremonies are more violent than many others at the Workshops, they are not entirely dissimilar. Other tales of various humiliating and unsafe activities included ducking in water, welding boots to the floor and, in one particularly horrible case, extreme persecution that included a mock rape, build up an unsavoury image of life for apprentices in Western Australia's largest industrial factory in the latter decades of the twentieth century. It is interesting to compare the initiation stories from the Midland Railway Workshops with those of a contemporary workplace, the East Perth Power Station. While some interviewees from both workplaces conceded that these practices would be regarded as bullying and sexual abuse today, few of those interviewed reflected upon the emotional and physical risks of initiation practices. Some even blamed the victims for not accepting it in the 'right spirit'.

These accounts raise many questions. What was the rationale for justifying the practice? If initiations were harmless rituals, why were the interviewees prepared to discuss their experiences as victims but not as perpetrators? Why did management turn a blind eye? Why did some foremen openly permit victimisation? Is initiation a thing of the past, or do these practices still flourish in particular workplaces? Before seeking answers to these questions, I will define initiations and pranks, and the difference between them.

Differences between and initiations and pranks

Apprentices were subject to two types of humiliating practices: initiations and pranks. Initiations were ordeals (sometimes extremely elaborate) that a boy was forced to go through, usually by older apprentices and often in the first year of his apprenticeship, in order to be accepted as one of the elite trade for which he was being trained. In his history of the Amalgamated Engineering Union, Sheridan referred to the importance of these rituals as 'rites of passage', usually a once-only, sometimes extremely elaborate ordeal. Many of the older tradesmen regarded the initiation as a necessary means of teaching the apprentice a lesson. A common attitude expressed at the Workshops and the power station was that apprentices were 'cheeky little buggers' who deserved to be taken down a peg or two. This, coupled with the workplace code of silence, ensured that perpetrators almost always got away with it. The tradesmen, foremen and even management usually turned a blind eye.

Pranks, on the other hand, could be played on anybody as long as he wasn't senior to the perpetrators. Tradesmen often played relatively harmless pranks on apprentices, such as sending them to the shop for striped paint, a box of square holes, a long 'weight' [wait], and so forth, or on individuals or groups of members of another trade. The latter usually occurred before Christmas at the Workshops when everyone went a bit crazy in the last couple of days before the two week holiday break. Mates played pranks on each other. Apprentices also played pranks on each other, and on certain marginalised individuals who were regarded as lower in the pecking order than apprentices: labourers and junior workers, never tradesmen or the foreman. While an examination of pranks helps to balance the picture and show that apprentices were certainly not always the victims, it is the concept, practice and rationale for the initiation ceremony that is the focus of this chapter.

Some initiation ceremonies were brief, involving one or more of the following: dousing with a fire hose, stripping naked, anointing with some foul substances such as graphite grease or dye that took many weeks to completely expunge, locking up in a confined space such as the smoke box or boiler of a steam locomotive, sometimes while other apprentices

The Peanut King initiation ceremony was possibly unique to Midland. These images show the 'Peanut' with his crown and tie seated on a platform in front of the tender and then being dumped on as the Master of Ceremonies flees. (Photos courtesy of Fred Cadwallader.)

hammered on the outside and throwing into a rubbish-filled pit. At the power station, this seemed to be the limit of the initiation experience. Michael Goff, a former employee, recalled: 'Everybody would have a good old laugh, slap on the back and into the showers.'

The Peanut King

At the Workshops, a far more elaborate initiation ceremony developed over the years and was practised (with variations) in a number of shops on the Midland site, including the foundry, the paint shop, the fitting shop and the machine shop. In some forms, it involved only one boy, in others, several. This ceremony, known as the Peanut King, may have been unique to the Midland Railway Workshops. Peanut King ceremonies began in the late 1930s and were still being practised in the 1960s, but not, it seems, by the 1970s when Stephen Smith began his apprenticeship. Compared with some of the assaults perpetrated, particularly in later years, what actually happened at the Peanut King ceremony was relatively mild, as it did not involve stripping naked or life-threatening behaviours, but it was designed to be a very public humiliation.

Here is Jack Emery's description of an early form of the Peanut King involving several boys in the machine shop where he worked during the 1930s.

> Christmas was … the time for apprentices to have some high jinks. The infamous Peanut Club involved the older apprentices going around the new apprentices asking for promises of donations to a mythical Xmas peanut fund. To give this operation credibility they also approached the tradesmen who responded with generous promises of money, which were added to the list in front of the unknowing new apprentices. On peanut day the most gullible new boys were gathered on a platform erected against an empty locomotive tender in which lurked unseen, a group of older apprentices armed with sloppy lagging, old tins of oil, and foul slops of any kind. A large crowd gathered to hear the new boys read out lists of promised donations which they [the audience] cheered or booed according to the amount pledged.
>
> The din was terrific, so nobody heard any noises coming from the villains behind the platform and concealed in the tender. In the middle of the new boys' performance, all the gathered filth and garbage was poured over the side of the tender onto the unfortunate Peanuts below. When they ran out of ammunition a large fire hose was turned on those who had not fled. After this there was a fight for the hose which became a free for all, with the hose and the remaining garbage as weaponry. When the fight for the hose began, the assembled crowd of adults would melt away and leave the apprentice mob to fight it out.

A 1950s Peanut King ceremony in the foundry involved one victim, who was encouraged to dress in a good shirt and tie and to wear a crown and carry a sceptre fashioned for him by his workmates. Fred Cadwallader recalled that there was a crown, specially made for the occasion and that

> Another year, another one of them even had a sceptre, a crown and a sceptre. There was some kind of a globe protector or something [for the crown], it was like a dome shape with ribs of metal in, it had a kind of peak on it but it just fitted a bloke's head. So, 'Hey this will do for the Peanut King', someone said, and for several years there they [used] this crown. You had to dress him up, too. He's had to bring a tie, you know, even

though he has got his working shirt on.

Also, in the foundry ceremony, according to Cadwallader, the boy might actually be given some of the pledges as a donation of money that he could spend on himself. The paint shop ceremony involved apprentices climbing onto the roof of the building and tipping paint on the unfortunate peanut below.

How the workers explained initiation practices

While some workers viewed the Peanut King ritual with distaste, others saw merit in it. Bob Wells, a car and wagon builder at the Workshops from 1963 until 1977, did not see the Peanut King as a victim, rather as someone who understood and worked the system to his advantage. Wells believed that the Peanut King was not 'harmful to the individuals' and that the apprentices were not forced into it. Instead, he thought that it was just 'a part of growing up' and assimilating into the Workshops environment. 'It certainly wasn't the case of targeting some poor slow individual and it did have to do with how they fitted into the social fabric of the shop itself.' Wells' assessment contrasts with the opinions of other workers. Ivan McMillan, for example, who was an apprentice mechanical fitter during the second half of the 1940s, recalled the Peanut King as 'the most highly organised and well-publicised scam squarely aimed at gullible apprentices'. Similarly, Fred Cadwallader was emphatic that the apprentice picked for the honour was, 'Usually the youngest one who wasn't a wake up. The second year [apprentices] had already gone through it. Whether they were selected or not they'd seen the peanut king crowned so they did not want to be in that.'

McMillan's and Cadwallader's assessments agree with the comments of some other former apprentices, who, far from seeing themselves as the star of the show, looked forward with the utmost dread to such occasions. Alan Wahl began as a junior worker in the chief mechanical engineer's office in 1935. Although he did not mention the Peanut King in his memoir, he wrote of his relief at being selected to work as a clerk in an environment that he depicted as clean and genteel, especially when compared to the tough atmosphere of the Workshops floor. Apparently, there was not the slightest suggestion that clerical workers went through any rites of passage, whereas stories of initiations on the factory floor filled Wahl with dread.

While these stories were probably grossly exaggerated, I did not relish the thought of being forced to participate in any way – particularly as victim. The thought of having to leave the comfort of serving in the Office, a job I had come to enjoy, had no appeal at all and I viewed the approach of the end of my six months with some apprehension.

Rod Quinn, an apprentice car and wagon builder from 1950 to 1956, also commented on 'cruelty in the form of hostile teasing, initiations and even physical bullying' practised by younger members of the workforce, including locking apprentices in a confined, noisy space that was attacked from the outside with hammers. Apprentices quickly learnt that you had to be able to take a joke or else, as former apprentice painter Geoff Hutchison recalled. You had to 'be able to take it as well as give it. Never crack if you were the recipient of a prank.' Hutchison learnt 'to always have an answer for anything (guilty or not). Be ever vigilant and never lose your temper.'

Hutchison's, King's, Quinn's and Wahl's experiences indicate that there was a very strong element of bullying and harassing the weak and vulnerable at the Railway Workshops. The older apprentices, in particular, sensed a victim and in King's experience the tradesmen joined in. Macmillan also recalled that 'tricks' (by which he probably meant the pranks that others referred to) were played on 'naïve apprentices' and that in each 'fresh crop ... the likely ones were soon identified and tested for vulnerability'.

This bullying element seemed to be much less in evidence at the East Perth Power Station, probably because the workforce was quite small and there is only slight evidence of the fierce intertrade rivalries that occurred at the Workshops. Even relationships between white- and blue-collar workers were of mutual respect, quite unlike the mutual hostility expressed between factory workers and clerical staff at Midland. Time keeper Kevin Mountain recalled that any clerical staff member who dared come onto the factory floor risked having his white shirt pelted with red dirt, and former apprentice Mae Jean Parker said, 'You never spoke to anyone in a white shirt'. In general, the power station initiations seemed closer to the pranks that Workshops apprentices experienced than to full initiations. Boilermaker Michael Goff, who did his apprenticeship at the power station, reflected that 'If you were an extremely sensitive person obviously it may have affected you', and admitted that 'if it was done today, you would all go to jail', but in those days 'it was an accepted practice that the tradespeople had gone through probably since stonemasons started'.

One characteristic common to the two workplaces was the need for apprentices to maintain solidarity in the face of punishment. Goff recalled a prank that went wrong when an unsuspecting bystander, who happened to wear a hearing aid, copped a bucket of water intended for another apprentice. As none of the apprentices would own up, the engineer in charge punished them all by taking a small sum out of each pay packet to pay for a new hearing aid.

While some attitudes expressed towards initiations seem casual, even cruel, one has to place them in the context of the workplace. Prior to the 1970s, employees at the Railway Workshops had little in the way of safety equipment, and even what was available was often rejected. Neil McDougall, an apprentice fitter in the 1960s, recalled working with asbestos: 'no breathing apparatus or anything', no protection from noise.

> That was another culture too – I don't know whether it was fostered by management or the men. You were expected to grin and take it. When they brought the first masks in, the guys wouldn't wear them: sissies. Ear muffs? Sissies. By the late 1960s – early '70s, stuff was starting [to come] in and health and safety [were] mandatory. Management ... wasn't refusing to bring it in; they did bring it in. Their biggest problem was getting people to use it ... And as for injuries. Well, it was heavy industry: cuts, bruises, all sorts of things were a daily [occurrence]. It was no big deal if you got your finger flattened or split.

Perhaps the most surprising thing is that the Workshops was open for ninety years and employed up to 3500 workers at one time, yet while there were thousands of accidents ranging from splinters, bruises and squashed or split fingers, to lost limbs, there were only twenty-two recorded fatalities, and most of these occurred prior to 1940, the last being in 1967. Consequently, there is some logic in understanding risky and humiliating practices as simply part and parcel of life in a dangerous, masculine work place. Women did not work on the factory floor until 1989, but when they began training as apprentices, they, too experienced these rituals.

Interviewees: victims, never perpetrators

While some of the workers interviewed for the History Projects about the two workplaces laughed off the effects of initiations, and others admitted that the practices were abhorrent, frightening and violent, few admitted to actually being perpetrators. In the worst case, that of the mock rape, the narrator actually distanced himself by saying, 'I felt so sorry for that kid', but he did nothing to stop it.

This reluctance to accept responsibility suggests that many of those interviewed knew that some of the initiations went beyond the bounds of a bit of fun, that some victims were injured and that the emotional effects were often quite traumatic. Initiations are always carried out by a group or gang upon a minority – perhaps one, perhaps a few. What, in the heat of the moment and the context of the group and the workplace, may seem acceptable behaviour, looks quite different several decades later in the light of contemporary awareness of the impact of bullying and bastardisation. I suspect that some of the men were ashamed of their conduct and did not wish to admit it. Some would go no further than saying there were a few pranks and practical jokes played, disliking the term 'initiation', as this excerpt from my interview with Kevin Wulff, an electrical fitter at the East Perth Power Station, shows:

> Interviewer: What about pranks and initiations and things? Was there at any point in the apprenticeship a feeling that you had to go through some kind of trial or initiation in order to be accepted?
>
> Wulff: I think there was probably ... there were pranks played against ... new apprentices. Nothing ominous or frightening or anything like that. But there were certainly pranks played against first year apprentices.
>
> Interviewer: Do you remember any in particular?
>
> Wulff: No I can't remember any actually off hand.
>
> Interviewer: The long wait or ...?
>
> Wulff: Well, yes, well, I mean, [there] were those sorts of things, like the tradesman used to send the junior apprentice away for a long wait and things like that. There were others that I can't recall off hand but, yes, there were things like that were played on new apprentices.

So, he would admit to the harmless pranks but not anything more serious – if it occurred – which other interviews suggest was the case.

Why did management turn a blind eye?

Given that, for most of its period of operation, Workshops management was drawn from the factory floor, managers knew very well what took place, as they had served apprenticeships either in Midland or a similar factory. So this question could be aimed at factory management anywhere. Initiations were a widespread practice in the Workshops environment and elsewhere, even into the present day, as recurring scandals about bastardisation of military recruits have revealed. Observance of occupational health and safety requirements, and the increased numbers of women in the workplace have contributed to breaking the code of silence that has surrounded these practices. Previously, it seemed, management regarded initiations as just part of an apprentice's education.

Perhaps more surprising is the fact that some foremen openly permitted victimisation, as evidenced in this story told by Steve Smith of the boy who was mock raped. The assault in this case was led by a tradesman who had threatened the boy, 'I'm going to get you one day.' After the assault, the boy complained to his mother, who came to the Workshops the next day and lodged a complaint with the foreman. The foreman brought in the perpetrators and gave them a dressing down in front of the apprentice and his mother. Then, after the mother departed, the foreman – not the tradesman who had committed the assault, but the foreman – turned to the boy and said, 'You have just signed your own death warrant'. If Smith's recollection is correct, the foreman was inviting the other workers to continue and even step up their persecution. The physical and psychological abuse continued until the boy was forced to leave.

Is initiation a thing of the past?

This incident of the boy and the mock rape occurred in the 1970s. When asked about initiations, some Workshops and power station former employees stated that it would not happen today because either the perpetrators would land in serious trouble – possibly even face a prison sentence for assault – or because people simply 'wouldn't put up with it'. Yet, as Mae Jean Parker's crucifixion experience shows, people were still being subjected to humiliating practices in the early 1990s. These days, laws ensure some form of protection against bullying or bastardisation, but getting redress in such circumstances, as a number of publicised cases have shown, is still no easy matter. One cannot help wondering how many workers continue to suffer in silence for fear of losing their job, rather than seek the legal protection that is their right.

The research indicates that almost all of apprentices who trained at the Midland Government Railway Workshops and probably most of those at the East Perth Power Station went through some form of initiation ceremony. Most survived the experience and put it behind them, a few managed to avoid it, and another few could not cope with the experience and either left or in one case purportedly took her own life. Did it do the majority any harm? Probably. But as with some emotional or physical injuries, they gradually healed or scarred over until it didn't seem to matter as much. Were initiations necessary to the discipline and training of these young people? Surely not.

How is this part of the culture interpreted?

Initiations, pranks and bullying were, regrettably, part of the culture of the Workshops. Consequently, whatever means are used to interpret the Workshops spaces' have to include this darker side of the culture. There are many photographs and a considerable amount of audio devoted to the Peanut King, and other interviews and written memoirs that mention other forms of initiation. Video of Mae Jean Parker relating her crucifixion experience is part of the archive.

How should these tools be used?

Currently, the main means of interpretation is by panels describing activities at certain sites, such as the flagpole, the peace memorial and the CME's office. Should panels be erected in the foundry or the paint shop to describe the Peanut King ritual? In the main blocks or other parts of the site to indicate spots where initiations took place? The MRA and its successor the MetRA commissioned a number of statues for parts of the site. None of these directly relate to the work. They are not, for example, comparable with the life-like statues in Fremantle depicting fishermen at work, immigrant children arriving at the quay, or the commercial traveller being threatened by a dog. How wonderful it would be to have a statue depicting the final moments of the Peanut King ceremony, where the apprentices rise out of the locomotive tender with buckets of filth to tip on the head of the unwary peanut below. This would certainly spark the interest of passers-by as well as visitors to the site. A site panel placed nearby could explain the action. What a story that would be.

5
Political Activity at the Midland Railway Workshops

Apart from the industrial activism that made the site a battleground between bosses and workers, the Workshops was the stage for other kinds of political activity. Several Labor politicians began their working life and developed their political activism there, including Ron Davies, state ALP leader from 1978 to 1981. But the political party that made the most impact on the day to day life of Workshops' employees was, arguably, the one that made the least impact on parliamentary politics – the Communist Party of Australia (CPA). Although a small minority among the workforce at the Workshops in the 1950s, the communists formed an active group whose physical focal point was Red Square, that section of the machine shop in Block 3 where CPA member Jack Marks, a fitter and turner, operated a heavy Dean and Grace lathe. Marks and his fellow communists were very active in achieving better working conditions, hence their political and industrial influence upon other unionists was significant.

In 1950, the year that the federal government passed legislation to ban the CPA, Rod Quinn entered his training as an apprentice car and wagon builder at the Workshops. According to Quinn, 'On the face of it, international events barely affected life in the Workshops [and] life there also barely affected international events', yet he described his six years at Midland as the birth of his activism. Among the workforce, he met men from all over the world, including a former Red Army soldier and prisoner of war, who taught him a few words of Russian. This man, exiled from his homeland by Stalinist policies, must have seen a grim irony in Quinn chalking 'Stalin the Teacher' and 'other absurdities' in Russian on the sides of wagons.

'Bullshit Castle'. The Chief Mechanical Engineer's Office, 2001. (Photo courtesy of Mia Lindgren)

Communist activity at the Workshops in the 1950s centred on Red Square. Here, within easy sight of the machine shop foreman's office. Jack Marks proselytised about communism to his fellow workers during his lunchtime. Marks was also an active unionist whose popularity among the wider workforce was despite, rather than because of, his communist beliefs.

Midland was the last of the major railway workshops to be built in Australia in the mid to late nineteenth and early twentieth centuries.

It is beyond the scope of this study to ascertain whether communists were significantly active in all of these factories during the interwar and Cold War periods. According to rail historian Lucy Taksa, Stan Jones, a communist shop committee and Australian Railways Union (ARU) member, placed great emphasis on the importance of Eveleigh Railway Workshops' 2600 workers to the political and industrial development of the NSW labour movement in 1939. This has echoes at Midland although, prior to World War II, communists played an insignificant role in that development. The Left–Right factional struggles that gripped the Amalgamated Engineering Union (AEU) from the 1940s to the 1960s no doubt also impacted upon every workplace where that union had significant representation. At Midland, the AEU was one of the four largest unions and perhaps the most militant. A number of studies of the labour movement depict the 1950s as an ideological battleground at national, state and regional level.

Even in the Depression and post-World War II eras, when communists had a massive impact upon eastern states' labour movements, in the Western Australian labour movement, conservative views dominated. The moderate parliamentary Labor Party was in government for all but three years in the period from 1924 to 1947. Conversely, the CPA, founded in 1920, struggled to maintain even a minute membership. There was no independent trades and labour council, therefore, no forum for unions or unionists who were not affiliated with the ALP, which consisted of a political and an industrial wing united in one body. As a result, the great majority of the state's unions and unionists were affiliated with the ALP. The AWU dominated this body until after World War II. Affiliates had to swear allegiance to the ALP, and union officials who belonged to other political parties were not permitted to attend meetings of the ALP's District Councils, thus seriously disadvantaging the unions they represented. After World War II, the increase in numbers and influence of several militant unions (for example, the AEU, the Collie Miners Union and the Waterside Workers' Federation), the decline in numbers and influence of the conservative AWU, and the state ALP's loss of government in 1947 (see chapter 7) were significant factors leading to the eventual formation of an independent TLC in 1963. In this hostile context, the achievements of a small cell of communist workers within the state's largest industrial workplace may be of more historical significance than it might have been in an environment in which the CPA had more influence.

Communist activity: 1930s and 1940s

True to the moderate nature of the Western Australian labour movement, Kathy Bell's interwar study of the Midland Railway Workshops reveals a politically and industrially conservative workforce, with a significant proportion of British tradesmen (see chapter 3). The WA Amalgamated Society of Railway Employees (WAASRE), the numerically dominant union, was moderate, although Bell indicates that the Midland Junction Branch was 'on the radical wing'. The AEU and the Boilermakers, on the other hand, were militant unions, with the AEU state branch being possibly 'the most militant in Australia'. According to Bell, 'oral evidence supports the view that there was a degree of leftist influence in the workshops', with one of the workers who she interviewed recalling that, although they were only a small minority, 'there was a definite Communistic crowd'. At the beginning of World War II, there were only about 300 CPA members in Western Australia. The federal government's national ban of the members in June 1940 resulted in police raids on homes, arrests and the imprisonment of several leaders. After the Curtin Labor Government lifted the ban in 1942, and while Russia enjoyed the status of wartime ally, the CPA's membership increased to an estimated 25,000 nationwide, 1500 of whom were in Western Australia. Despite the Party's insignificant presence in the state, Western Australians voted in favour of a ban on the CPA in the 1951 referendum. As the Cold War descended upon the postwar world, the union movement in Australia divided into warring communist and anti-communist camps, which, as Sheridan showed, sometimes fractured individual unions. The ALP dissociated itself from the CPA in a series of resolutions, ultimately permitting the passage through the Senate of legislation to again ban the Party.

The communists also suffered from their association with several bitter, unsuccessful postwar industrial disputes. One such dispute erupted after the October 1951 national decision by Commonwealth Conciliation Commissioner J. M. Galvin not to increase metal workers' margins. This was purportedly an attempt to prevent inflation, but it incensed the unions involved. Historian Jan Archer argued that although the Galvin decision did not directly affect metal trades workers in Western Australia, who came under a separate (higher) state award, union activists used it as the catalyst for what became the longest-running strike in Western Australian industrial history. Communists were prominent among these activists. Archer's emphasis on the role played by Marks, Jack Coleman and other CPA members at the Workshops during the six months strike, is confirmed by oral and written sources. Communist-linked groups, such as the Modern Women's Club, organised lunches and sewing bees for the strikers' families. But the communist presence was also a disadvantage, which apparently was instrumental in the strike's failure. With the Right-wing unions – in particular the giant WAASRE with 900 Workshops' members – refusing to join in, the smaller AEU and the Boilermakers had little hope of success. Some union secretaries warned their members against attending meetings in connection with the Double the Margins campaign – as it became known – because they believed it was communist-inspired. Consequently, despite widespread community support, nothing was achieved by the strike and, according to some former employees, not only did many Midland workers become even more hostile to the communist members in their midst, but they also became disillusioned about the promises made by unions. As the factory was a closed shop, each worker had to belong to a union, but even though they were union members, many played no role in union activities. How then did active communist unionists such as Coleman and Marks make an impact on this largely sceptical workforce?

The role of communist agitators

Dedicated communists appear to have impressed their fellow workers because they were competent tradesmen and committed unionists. In their roles as shop stewards, they worked hard to obtain better pay and conditions. Some had considerable personal skills of oratory, persuasion and humour. According to Jack Marks' biographer, Jolly Read, Jack Coleman recalled that 'Wherever there were communists in industry they were never criticised for their work. They were not loafers and were very honest people in that regard.' Thus, although few workers at Midland embraced the communist philosophy, communists as a group began to exert a significant influence in the workplace. Owen Salmon, who often visited the Workshops in his role as state organiser for the Electrical Trades Union (ETU), commented that there was 'virtually a communist cell' at Midland. The members were veterans of the 1952 strike, who continued to work for improvements in this

Dickensian workplace, despite the failure of the Double the Margins campaign and their subsequent unpopularity.

The activities of Red Square were closely linked with the public space around the flagpole in front of Block 1. Erected in 1916 as a temporary memorial to Workshops employees who died on active service in World War I, the flagpole was relocated to its site outside Block 1 in 1924, prior to the construction of the permanent peace memorial. The flagpole soon became a focus for workers' gatherings when there were grievances to discuss, as well as a forum for parliamentarians, political candidates and other public figures wishing to address the assembled workforce. It was the perfect platform for an orator. Marks was popular as a flagpole speaker. Coleman said that

> There would be a flagpole meeting on ... and people would ask if Marksy was speaking. He would come back from deputations over at the main office, which he called bullshit castle, and say things like 'Well apart from an aching anus, I got nothing!' It appealed to the blokes.

The Workshops was very territorial. By referring to the CME's office as Bullshit Castle, Marks was cleverly playing on the class divisions between white- and blue-collar workers. Although many workers passed from trades to clerical, after studying to become engineers or draftsmen – and at least three men worked their way up from being junior workers to CME of the Workshops – the site itself was demarcated into blue-collar and white-collar territory, and within that into the territory of the individual trades. Foundry worker Fred Cadwallader described the intense rivalry between workers in the foundry and the boiler shop. It was also a site of gendered spaces. Until the late 1980s, the only female spaces were the canteen and the CME's office. There had been a casualty room nursing sister, known unflatteringly as Iodine Annie, but she was replaced by a male attendant in 1950. The flagpole and Red Square were spaces with dual or multiple meanings – the ones for which they were originally intended, any further uses vested upon them by management, and the appropriated uses to which the workers put them. Red Square, in particular, gained its own mythology, so that employees who joined the Workshops long after Marks had left recalled what went on there.

After the closure of the Workshops in 1994, and during subsequent redevelopment and reinterpretation of the site, Red Square featured on heritage walks, with former employee guides delighting in pointing out its proximity to the foreman's office. But in traversing the empty, open spaces of the disused workshop today, it is difficult to construe the power struggles that made this spot so significant, and easy to lose the real meaning of Red Square.

Increasingly, heritage practitioners are becoming aware of the significance of power relations in the creation and adaptation of physical sites. In her study of the Victorian Trades Hall Council, Cathy Brigden discussed the power invested in that site, acquired in the 1850s as a place for the unions, and later, in the imposing trades hall building that became a dominant landmark. Brigden wrote: 'The idea that a place on the map is also a place in history underscores the spatial and temporal significance of the [Melbourne] Trades Hall.' In the vicinity of Red Square, the structure that most represented managerial power was the elevated foreman's office. Its occupant, the foreman, was 'one of us' who had become 'one of them'. In order to understand the full significance of the communists' bravado, it is necessary to appreciate the attitudes of shop floor workers to the foremen, their superiors and fellow tradesmen, who they regarded as policemen and objects of suspicion. According to Dave Hicks, a fitter and turner who worked in Red Square during the 1970s:

> The senior foreman's office … would be elevated and he could see right down each end of the [machine] shop; he could stand in his window and watch what's happening. And the clerk would always be up there. So, if you wanted to get out of the joint, if you needed to go to the doctor or you were feeling sick, you would have to go up to the clerk and ask for a pass, a leave pass. It was like a jail. The control they exercised in that place was absolute.

Irrespective of their personal political beliefs, most of workers in the machine shop would have relished verbal battles between Marks and Leo McNamara, foreman fitter during the latter part of the 1950s, who was known to be a strict Catholic and who may have belonged to the Democratic Labour Party (DLP), the conservative section of the ALP that formed a new party after splitting from the main party in 1955.

Many past employees had fond memories of Marks. Phillip Bristow Stagg, a turner and iron machinist, recalled that Marks had got him involved in the AEU. He felt that if Marks had joined the ALP instead of the CPA, he would have become a member of parliament because 'he could talk people into anything'. Patrick Gayton, a pattern maker, also said that Marks was 'a great orator' who 'could talk us into anything really. He was funny, he used to [say]... "Have you seen the daily sausage wrapper today?" [meaning] ... the *West Australian*, of course.'

Even Ron Wadham, who was works manager between 1978 and 1989, regarded Marks as 'a remarkable character ... a fine controller of men and a persuasive speaker. He would stand at Flagpole meetings and point towards the management buildings and decry the exploitation of the workers and pronounce the ineptitude of the manager.' Wadham was well aware of the power relationships in the Workshops, which he described as being 'a natural battleground'. His memoir is replete with phrases such as 'The troops [were] marching on the office' and 'The excitement of marching *en masse* to frighten me in my office soon lost its attraction'. He referred to Marks as 'a great guy and always good natured *outside the battle zone*' (my emphasis). It seems that Wadham regarded worker protest as a cynical game and thought that the union officials did likewise.

Irrespective of whether many employees shared Wadham's cynicism, the communist shop stewards appear to have been popular because they worked to improve conditions for the employees. Many of those interviewed referred to Dickensian conditions on the factory floor: inadequate washing and lunch time facilities, no safety gear, and noise, smoke and dirt, which made already dangerous working conditions even worse. Don Manning, who was a safety officer at the Workshops, said that despite years of agitation by the unions, many of these conditions prevailed until occupational health and safety legislation, passed in 1984, required management to adopt practices more appropriate to the late twentieth century, including enforcing the wearing of safety glasses, heavy boots, helmets, overalls and ear plugs, and investigating all incidents in which workers were injured.

Shop stewards Coleman and Marks operated in the unreformed atmosphere of the 1950s, when there were many causes for complaint. Coleman looked after the day to day needs of the blokes by ensuring that they received disability money for working in confined spaces and dirt money for working particularly dirty jobs, as well as other pay claims. According to Coleman, Midland was the first government workshops to get an industry allowance to compensate for workers being on award pay when private factories paid higher rates for the same skills. His strategy was to first discuss claims with the relevant foreman. 'Most foremen were good. I wouldn't argue or anything. They respect you if you recognise their position.' It was this reasonable attitude – far removed from popular contemporary images of fanatical communists – which no doubt won the respect of the foremen. Mutual respect extended beyond individual relationships. The Joint Railways Union Committee, on which communist and non-communist union officials cooperated to achieve improvements in the workplace, was frequently praised by the Workshops' own communist publication, *Unity*. In 1962, for example, *Unity* congratulated the Joint Railways Union Committee for the 'job they've done on behalf of workers in these Shops' and stated that the committee had been 'savaged by the DLP, the Employers' Federation and the monopoly press urging a return to unions going their separate ways'.

It would be incorrect, however, to impute that communists did not encounter prejudice and injustice because of their activities. The Workshops rules could be applied quite selectively, as they were when communist activist Norm Lacey, who had been employed for six months as a labourer, was dismissed on 11 May 1949 for 'breach of Workshops Rule 61, posting of unauthorised pamphlets in Workshops'. There were also sinister aspects to the way the communists operated. Edward King, a turner and iron machinist at the Workshops during the 1950s, regarded Marks as 'a genuine communist' – without elaborating on what 'a genuine communist' might mean to him – but despised 'the "red raggers" who trotted around in Jack's wake ... [who] would not know a communist if they fell over one'. King once complained to Marks because one of these red raggers had demanded money for the wharfies and, when King refused to contribute, started a rumour that he was 'scabbing on supporting the wharfies'. King claimed that he told Marks, 'I do not like people demanding money from me. If you want something from me, ask. Don't send your bully boys over to demand it.' Apparently, Marks agreed with him, and reprimanded the worker in question. It is not known whether this was an isolated case or a common practice.

Some ex-employees also spoke of interunion fighting or of power struggles within unions, involving communists, ALP and DLP members. Although there were DLP members among the Workshops employees, and some may have held roles in the executives of more conservative unions such as the Moulders, the ASE or the WAASRE, the DLP in Western Australia never developed a union base. Indeed, *Unity* rarely mentioned the DLP or 'groupers'. Groupers were members of so-called industrial groups that the DLP used to counter the influence of militant unions. But an article in the March 1955 issue did attack industrial groups, declaring that while this was not a sectarian issue it was concerned that employers used the groups to weaken and pacify the labour movement. Perhaps the DLP presence at Midland was insufficient to warrant further mention. If so, this would contrast with Sheridan's finding that, as early as 1938, the anti-communist movement found strong support among unionists in Victoria's railway workshops. Certainly, some workers at Midland expressed strong anti-communist views.

Perhaps the most revealing indicator of how workers regarded the communists in their midst may be the results of elections. Marks was elected repeatedly to the AEU executive and was branch president in the early 1960s. He was shop stewards' convenor at Midland Workshops, represented staff on the Punishments Appeal Board, and was the metal trades federal delegate. Evidently, people were less willing to have him represent them in parliament. Marks and other prominent communists such as Joan Williams and John Rivo Gandini stood for the House of Representatives and the Senate during various election campaigns in the 1950s and 1960s but none came close to victory. According to *Unity*, the communist vote increased in the federal electorate of Swan from 493 in 1959 to 801 in 1962 which, if accurate, indicates almost a doubling of support – but which sections of the electorate voted for communists is unknown. The residences of the Workshops workforce were widely scattered and it would be impossible to ascertain their impact on the vote.

Management's response

Workshops management appeared to have an ambivalent attitude to the presence of activists on the site. Anecdotal evidence suggests that known communist activists were not employed at the Workshops. Marks claimed that he was certain he would not get a job there even though he was qualified in his trade. On the day of his interview, the works manager was conducting a visitor around the Workshops and left the interview to his clerk, who did not know Marks. By the time management realised 'that they had let this dangerous red into the place it was too late because they were employing trainees and so they couldn't sack a tradesman'. (Trainees were adults who had not completed a trades apprenticeship, but who received trade training.) Thus Marks claimed to owe his position partly to luck and partly to the political and economic conditions prevailing after the war. Whether his recollection was accurate is unknown, but foremen's reports from the era attest to the extreme shortage of skilled tradesmen.

On entering employment at Midland, each employee was required to sign and abide by a set of Workshops rules, which were outlined in by-law 84 of the *Government Railways Act*. Copies of the Workshops rules were posted on walls in the various Workshops. Rule 61 prohibited canvassing, and Rule 62 forbade workers to hold meetings, take up collections, post notices or advertisements, or distribute literature of any kind without the permission of the works manager. Yet during the 1950s and 1960s *Unity* was distributed throughout the Workshops. The fact that *Unity* clearly stated that it was published by the Workshops Branch of the Communist Party of Australia and sometimes contained details of flagpole meetings to be held that same day indicates that it was handed out to workers as they arrived in the morning. This activity quite possibly occurred outside the main gate of the premises, but there is plenty of anecdotal evidence to indicate that workers regularly flouted the rules, most notably in making foreigners. With regard to management response to political activity, apart from the abovementioned sacking of Lacey, Dennis Day, a fellow communist and contemporary of Marks, who worked as a turner and iron machinist at the Workshops for twenty-four years, stated that he was sacked three times. On one occasion, he was sacked when he was accused of having copies of a banned book, *Portnoy's Complaint,* hidden at his house. CPA members had objected to the ban and sold copies of the book in the Pioneer Bookshop. In the other cases, Day appears to have been reinstated by union might and the threat of a strike in support of him.

Day also recalled an occasion where Works Manager Lucas Pitsikas, supported him against Machine Shop Foreman Leo McNamara. McNamara had refused to recognise Day as shop steward. Day claimed that McNamara, a devout Catholic who 'hated Comms', was forced by Pitsikas to recognise Day in his union role, despite his communist principles. This confrontation took place on the shop floor in front of the tradesmen and probably undermined McNamara's authority.

Although all flagpole meetings had to receive the works manager's prior permission, management did permit the use of a loud speaker and also allowed an electrical tradesman employed at the Workshops to set up the platform and amplification system in work time. By sanctioning properly organised flagpole meetings, management provided the workers with a means of letting off steam and airing legitimate industrial

When American singer and activist Paul Robeson was refused entry to the Workshops during his visit to Perth in 1960 he gave a concert to the workers from the back of a truck parked outside the perimeter fence. (Photo courtesy of Arnold Van Tongren)

grievances, but they also provided a platform for communists. A survey of *Unity* issues from the 1950s and 1960s indicates that communist candidates for state and federal elections, as well as those representing the major political parties, spoke at flagpole meetings on a number of occasions. Examples include Senate candidates Jack Marks and another well-known communist and militant union official, Paddy Troy, who addressed workers on 5 December 1961, and a meeting for communist candidates on 11 February 1965. In June 1958, Jim Healy, CPA member and federal secretary of the Waterside Workers' Federation, spoke at a lunch time gate meeting, which indicates that he was not permitted on the premises.

Better known is the refusal by Works Manager Bill Britter to permit American singer Paul Robeson to give a concert on the premises during his visit to Western Australia in December 1960. To the delight of hundreds of workers, Robeson defied the ban by performing on the back of a truck parked outside the perimeter fence. He then proceeded to a civic reception, hosted by the mayor of Midland, thus making the Workshops management look rather petty. According to Coleman, during the 1940s or 1950s, management banned flagpole meetings. After Bert Styants, Minister for Railways in then Premier Albert (Bert) Hawke's state Labor government (1953-59), intervened, the ban was revoked, but management stipulated that candidates speaking on behalf of political parties could address the workers only at election time. This may have been why Healy and Robeson were not permitted on the premises, whereas Troy, as a Senate candidate was.

Despite the large and fairly militant workforce, the Midland Railway Workshops was relatively free of industrial disputes. In the site's ninety-year history, only three strikes were commonly referred to: a dispute in 1912, the 1952 metal workers' strike and a stoppage during the 1970s over the issue of working with asbestos. Evidently, the union stewards' diligence in fighting for important issues, their access to management, irrespective of how negatively they represented these delegations at flagpole meetings, and the meetings themselves, were sufficient to defuse many potential strikes.

So, why did Marks, Coleman, Day and other communists enjoy such popularity at the Workshops? Thousands of workers, of many political persuasions, were committed to bettering their own conditions and those of their fellow workers long before, and after, communism became a recognised ideology in Australia. Marks was a particularly gifted and persuasive orator. It has been mentioned that some of the workers believed he could have had a long career in the parliamentary Labor Party, rather than joining the ALP in old age after his resignation from the CPA. Consequently, his political career was limited to local government, in which he served as inaugural mayor of Vincent (1995–98). Yet Marks influenced the lives of thousands of workers. He and the other communist shop stewards played prominent roles at Midland and in the Trades and Labor Council of Western Australia, and later became state organisers for their unions. Through their membership of the Joint Railway Unions Committee, they also influenced many other non-communist union officials and members, men such as Colin Hollett, Frank Bastow and Gordon Grenfell, some of whom also became state organisers. According to Jack Coleman, although his union, the WAASRE, barred him from its leadership because he was a communist, the men on the shop floor simply did not care about his politics as long as he achieved victories for them. He spoke of men coming up and congratulating him on making a stand against management and telling him that his adherence to communism would not make any difference to them.

As the CPA membership waxed and waned, it is evident that pragmatic Australian workers in the Midland Railway Workshops, as elsewhere, were prepared to accept the industrial benefits fought for by communist shop stewards, and to respect them as individuals, while emphatically rejecting their political ideology. Consequently, studying shop floor relations at the Workshops enables us to see communists working and cooperating with their fellow workers and management just as efficiently as did union officials of other political persuasions. In other words, the communists who devoted their working lives to bettering the pay and conditions of their fellow workers were, in general, regarded as being just ordinary people who cared about the welfare of others.

6
Technological Change at the Workshops, 1960s–1990s

According to the *Burra Charter*, the scientific or research value of a site depends upon 'the importance of the data involved, on its rarity, quality or representativeness, and on the degree to which the place may contribute to further substantial information'. Technological change is one means of demonstrating scientific value. The Midland Railway Workshops is a site where considerable technological change occurred, especially in its last three decades. This chapter identifies ways in which labour and labour processes from the 1960s to the 1990s were transformed at the Workshops by examining three major changes in technology and work practices during that time. It discusses ways these changes affected or influenced the apprenticeship and trades structure in the Workshops. These are the changes in work practices brought about by the move from steam to diesel locomotives, the introduction of new building materials such as fibreglass and aluminium to replace wooden wagons and carriages, and improved work safety practices. The chapter also discusses reforms to the apprenticeship system, including the shortening of trade apprenticeships from five to four years and employment of female apprentices.

The change from steam to diesel

Despite the phasing out of steam technology in the 1960s, the Workshops continued to be strongly associated with the age of steam. In 2001, for example, when media studies students at Murdoch University produced a CD featuring interviews with past employees, they chose to intersperse the interviews with the sounds of a steam locomotive whistling and shunting. Perhaps it was not inappropriate. For over two-thirds of its existence, the Workshops produced and maintained steam locomotives. The heyday of the Workshops was, arguably, from the 1940s to the 1960s, when the highest number of workers were employed, and unions and craft consciousness were strong. The steam era, too, seems to have left a deeper impression upon those who worked there across both periods. When asked about changes at the Workshops over their period of employment, many workers who commenced in the 1950s or earlier would not hesitate to say that the phasing out of steam locomotives and the introduction of diesels – a process that took over a decade – was the most profound change that they experienced.

The Workshops was designed to be a production line for the building and repair of steam locomotives. When a locomotive came in for an overhaul it arrived at the starting end, everything was pulled apart and cleaned and repaired before being re-assembled. During the course of an apprenticeship, irrespective of their ultimate trade, boys worked their way through the entire process and finished by knowing how the locomotives were constructed. The tradesmen with whom they worked, although specialists at their particular craft, be it boilermaking, fitting or coach building, were trained in the same way, but there was also a hierarchy of skill, or strong craft consciousness.

When the changeover from steam to diesel occurred at Midland, many of the workmen appeared to feel genuine regret about the loss of steam locomotives. This is curious, because the changeover happened at a time when modern progress was greatly desired and vaunted, while concepts such as heritage scarcely registered on the horizon of public consciousness. Lucas Pitsikas was a planner in the boiler shop in 1950, when the process of introducing diesel engines commenced. Pitsikas was sent to England to study designs for diesels. He was impressed by the generosity of the English designers, who gave him spare copies of their drawings. Pitsikas was, perhaps predictably, very positive about the change. Yet he recalled that many workers felt 'much sorrow', although they expressed little resistance to the advent of diesel engines despite a lengthy and difficult period of transition from steam, which ended in the late 1960s. Some workers left as a result of the change. Most received on the job training in handling diesels but the more ambitious augmented their practical work with study at night school, where Pitsikas taught tradesmen up to the level of foremen. Courses were available at the Railway Institute and at the Perth Technical College, where the lecturers

In the graveyard. A decommissioned L Class locomotive bound for scrap. (Photo courtesy of Nick Dragicevich)

included staff from The University of Western Australia. These courses adequately covered the requirements for tradesmen and theorists in the changeover from steam to diesel.

Steve Smith, who began as an apprentice boilermaker in 1972, in the final days of steam, recalled:

> [B]oilermakers ... were the king, they were the guys who built these steam engines and the fitters just used to fit the components, you know ... With the demise of steam, boilermakers now were structural workers. We were building wagons and bridges and all sorts of things. [With] diesel engines, the fitters became king. Now, we [boilermakers] used to call fitters boilermakers with their brains bashed out, and blacksmiths [we regarded as being] boilermakers who couldn't quite make the grade. Yeah, there was a lot that used to go on about which trade was more important or more skilled or more craft-like than the other, but I think it was during this period of transition from steam to diesel that the whole hierarchal

Even in the 1980s, when this photograph was taken, foundry workers wore a minimum of safety gear. The worker closest to the running stopper is wearing gloves, apron and face mask, but others further away are not even wearing gloves. (Photo courtesy of Fred Cadwallader)

structure of the Workshops changed. [Some trades vanished completely, for example] the laggers, the guys who used to lag steam locomotive boilers. With no steam there was no work. You saw other trades such as electronics begin to emerge; in the steam days there were no electronics, so you had this major shift occurring.

The effect of this removal of craft status was devastating for some workers. Blacksmiths, including Don Underdown, who was employed at the Workshops from 1949 until 1993, gained work in new areas but lost it elsewhere.

With dieselisation, the Workshops began making aluminium wagons instead of the old wooden ones. Thus, work that had traditionally required woodies' (carpenters') skills became blacksmiths' work. Blacksmiths had been going down the gurgler fast at this point because the skills required to refit a steam locomotive were no longer needed. When a steam loco came in for a refit, everything had to be cut off with an oxyacetylene torch, con rods lengthened or shortened, and wheels fitted with new tyres that had to be shrunk on by the blacksmiths before being machined. Initially, nothing ever fitted, so every little bracket had to be machined to fit. Consequently, the change to diesels meant a steep decline in the tasks performed by blacksmiths. According to Underdown, once the steamies went, the number of blacksmiths operating individual fires in the main shop declined from around eighty-seven to nineteen.

Table 1: Comparison of Trade Vacancies at the Midland Workshops 1940s and 1970s

Trade	1940–49	% vacancies	1970–79	% of vacancies
Boilermaker	219	15.0	172	11.0
Fitter (mechanical)	461	32.0	611	39.0
Fitter (electrical)	36	2.5	128	8.2
Turner and iron machinist	196	13.6	121	8.0
Blacksmith	36	2.5	75	4.8
Car and wagon builders	184	13.0	–	0.0
Painters	48	3.3	41	4.1
Scale adjuster	–		8	
Coach trimmers	15	1.0	14	0.9
Moulder	89	6.2	48	4.8
Motor mechanics	3		41	2.6
Coppersmith	22	1.5	25	1.6
Auto electrician	–		1	
Carpenter	–		7	
Wood machinist	6	0.4	8	0.55
Plumber	5	0.3	37	2.5
Electroplaters	–		7	
Sheetmetal worker	3	0.15	13	0.9
Pattern maker	11		8	
Trades recruited in numbers too small to be calculated as percentage		9.4		14.8
Total	**1439**	**100.0**	**1552**	**100.0**

The perception of a change in intake for the different trades is confirmed by the minutes of the Apprentices Application Board, which met annually to consider applications for apprenticeship vacancies. The preceding table indicates the changes in trades and the number of vacancies for trades between 1940 and 1979.

The most notable demise of any trade was that of the car and wagon builder, which constituted 13 per cent of the vacancies in the decade 1940–49 and none by the 1970s. Trades such as electrical fitters and plumbers, on the other hand, were increasingly in demand and between them constituted almost 11 per cent of vacancies for apprentices in the 1970s. Motor mechanics, similarly increased from three apprentices from 1940–49 to forty-one (or 2.6 per cent of the vacancies) from 1970–79. Adding to the unsettling of an environment that had long been regarded as stable and secure, other major changes were introduced in this decade.

Changes to the apprenticeship system

In the early 1970s, the trades apprenticeship was restructured and shortened from five to four years. Boys were accepted after completing their final year of high school, which meant that when they arrived at the Workshops to commence their training they were older and better educated than their predecessors. During the 1970s and 1980s, the entire class structure, based on the relationships between tradesmen and their trade assistants, apprentices and foremen, began to evolve into a quite different system, and by the late 1980s, the trades even began to admit female apprentices.

When Don Underdown started at the Workshops in March 1949 as an apprentice blacksmith, he found a rigid class system in which apprentices were expected to learn by watching the tradesmen. Often 'you just blundered along on your own'. An early task was learning to drive a steam hammer, which he was expected to learn in about a week, and 'then you're on your own'. The apprentice stood by the hammer 'not quite at attention but the next best thing to it. I believe in the early days they did stand to attention at the hammer.' When the blacksmith indicated he was ready, the apprentice lifted his hammer so that the white hot metal object could be placed underneath, and he would drive the hammer to forge the metal into the required shape. 'And God help you if you hit too hard and mucked it up; you'd get a belt across the ears. It was no use going to the boss and saying "He hit me", because when he came out they'd be waiting for you and they'd hit you again.' Underdown contrasted this with a later period when 'You daren't give an apprentice a backhander or, oh boy'.

Dave Moir's experience as an apprentice in 1977 was almost identical. Like Underdown, his first task was to master the steam hammer. He also stood all day and developed very sore legs from the effort.

> The first couple of weeks you had to be with this guy and you just had to stand there and watch and look ... and he told you about it and [then] you got to actually put the little grease thing in and grease up the ram on it and towards the end of the first week he'd let you put a block of wood under it and give it a bit of a tap and so by the time you come to the end of the fortnight you're able to hammer out a bit of metal.

Apart from the practical work, the apprentices got their share of book learning by attending the Midland Technical College one day a fortnight. Don Underdown later attended classes specifically for blacksmiths at Fremantle Technical College. He appreciated being able to make his own tools in the second year of his apprenticeship.

Bob Wells, who began his apprenticeship in 1963 as a car and wagon builder, saw no advantages in the shortened apprenticeship; it meant that boys were 'not fully trained' when they came onto the shop floor. Although the educational level was higher – boys were required to have their Leaving Certificate before applying – the four year apprenticeship in the electrical trades and fitting trades did not, Wells believed, 'provide the time for the apprentices to actually learn the significance of what they were doing'. Not only were these new apprentices 'not as dextrous as they ought to have been' but, in Wells' opinion they were also not well suited to the Workshops as their higher level of education made them look down on the trades people and, especially, the trades assistants. Unlike Underdown and Moir, Wells tended to support the old-fashioned method, whereby an apprentice observed the way that his tradesman performed a task, and then did it in exactly the same way. He believed that the apprentices who came after completing high school failed to understand that the 'education they were about to receive on the shop floor was a physical education in how the work was to actually be done'. Instead, 'they tended to look for answers out of books as to how a tradesman did their work and that's not how tradesmen work'.

Bill Kirkham, master of apprentices from 1974 to 1988, was similarly sceptical about the value of the extra two years at high school.

> Most of our apprentices were from year 10, some year 11 and 12 also. With the year 12s we found that they were not smarter than the year 10s ... In some cases, it only showed that their parents were able to afford to keep their kids at school for another two years. A lot of [the Year 12s] thought the trades were a bit tedious and they would much rather be involved in the professional side such as becoming academics and bank managers, whereas the Year 10 – all he wanted to do was something with his hands, none of this academic stuff.

Even so, Kirkham believed that the Year 12 graduates had greater maturity and capability and he encouraged them to enter the more demanding trades such as electrical and mechanical fitting and to study for a diploma or degree so that they could qualify as a draughtsman and later as an engineer. During the time that he was Master of Apprentices, Kirkham opened nine new apprentice schools to cater for far more than the original basic skilling, and he appointed young instructors who developed a good rapport with the boys. One class rebuilt a 1927 fire engine, which was later placed in the Western Australian Museum. Others assisted in building the *SS Leeuwin*. The Workshops strongly encouraged apprentices to gain relevant educational qualifications. Nick Dragicevich, for example, stated that Westrail was 'a very forward organisation for its time in that it encouraged apprentices to go to night school and to take on additional studies in drawing and drafting'. He put his own success down to the encouragement of Luke Pitsikas who advised him to learn to be a draftsman.

The other major change in the apprenticeship system occurred when females were permitted to commence apprenticeships. This was a government requirement as part of its equal opportunity legislation. Very few females took up this challenge and only two completed their apprenticeship. Sindy Hunter graduated on the eve of the Workshops' closure; Mae Jean Parker completed her apprenticeship elsewhere. Although she could not obtain a job in private enterprise after the closure, Hunter recalled her apprenticeship at the Workshops as a happy and fulfilling time. She stated that the older tradesmen 'looked after' the female apprentices and were 'like fathers' to them. Her account was in stark contrast to the experiences suffered by many of the male apprentices only a decade or so earlier at the hands of older apprentices and the younger tradesmen (see chapter 4), and also with Parker, whose experience is discussed below.

Occupational health and safety

A third major change in the Workshops was the introduction of more comprehensive safety measures, some of which stemmed from the passage in the WA parliament of the 1984 *Occupational Health and Safety Act*. During the 1980s, the Trades and Labor Council of Western Australia made a major commitment to improving safety on worksites. The TLC's commitment to occupational health and safety (OHS) issues was most clearly demonstrated by its appointment of Stephanie Mayman as OHS officer in 1983, and an industrial democracy officer, Tim Noonan, in 1984. Noonan's duties included assisting Mayman to prepare OHS information for unions, prior to the introduction of state government policy that would give workers a greater role in promoting health and safety in the workplace. Mayman and the TLC executive led a full-scale campaign to improve workplace safety. The campaign was launched partly in response to the finding that exposure to blue asbestos in mining townships such as Wittenoom was a direct cause of various forms of cancer. Wittenoom had been closed in 1978, although the state government of Sir Charles Court investigated the possibility of moving the town to a nearby location, until it was realised that the health hazard was too great. The TLC campaigned to remove asbestos from worksites (including the Workshops) and to gain compensation for the victims of asbestos-related diseases. Workshops employees commented on the minimal health and safety practices. Nick Dragicevich admitted putting off having an X-ray because he feared what it might reveal as a result of his exposure to asbestos. Boilermaker Graeme Bywater also mentioned his exposure to asbestos while working in the salvage section of the Workshops.

Prior to 1949, welders were the only workers to wear gloves. Then some of the European immigrants introduced gloves and other employees began to see the benefits and started getting their own. The blacksmiths would get old welders' gloves and cut a piece out of them so that they slid over the hand and could be flipped back if a man needed to use his fingers. The only protective gear was a leather apron, heavy boots – not steel capped safety boots – and a hat. No goggles or ear muffs were worn, despite the fact that most accidents occurred to the eyes and that the working environment was often extremely noisy, resulting in many employees suffering from industrial deafness.

Blacksmith Dave Moir recalled that, in 1977, earmuffs were still not available, so he was most affected by working in the spring shop setting leaf springs.

> You used to hold the leaf springs with a pair of tongs and then your striker would hit it with a big sledge hammer and it wasn't done red hot, it was just warmed up so, being spring steel, being hard and tempered, it would really ring and give this high-pitched ring so when you're bashing away doing all these leaves you had to do a quota of so many sets of springs per day. When I worked up there it was the worst because I would go home and hear this constant ringing in my ears. It wasn't until later on [that] I realised it was all the banging and banging 'cause when I worked elsewhere I didn't have the problem, but I s'pose the damage was already done by then.

Workers provided their own clothes because no uniforms were issued by Westrail until years later. Moir remarked that the Workshops 'improved a lot in 17 years' – that is, by 1994 when the closure occurred.

Similarly, when Don Manning arrived at the Workshops as a 15 year old apprentice in 1947, safety and sanitary standards were very poor. 'When I started work if you were the person wearing gloves, you were a poofter and if you were wearing glasses, you are a faggot.' When he left forty-three years later, 'the environment was very good ... because it had to comply with the *OHS Act* – eating rooms, all the protective equipment you could wish for'. Originally, workers had to heat their own water to wash in. Some would leave dirty water for others, some would urinate in the water (until it was like 'pee soup'), still others would never change their clothes. Manning knew of one man who bought new overalls at the beginning of the year and discarded them, unwashed, at the end of the year.

Manning testified to the fact that the OHS legislation was directly responsible for changed practices as the Workshops was obliged to comply with the Act's requirements. Because so many trades were present, the involvement of the whole Workshops community was necessary to build a safe working environment, and this included the appointment of safety representatives who liaised with union representatives and the safety officer, and the organisation of safety training for workers. Manning admitted that, even in later years, it was

> very hard to get people involved because they always think that they know all about it. It was hard and it was a challenge ... It's a matter of changing attitudes and that's why they have safety awards for the staff to make them take safety seriously. Lots of chaps have said to me that outside [businesses] have no safety compared to the Workshops where they used to work before.

As safety officer, Manning, who had an advisory role, was in frequent contact with the Department of Occupational Health and Safety to obtain advice and information on problems as they arose. When Manning commenced his duties in 1979–80, among a staff of 2500, there were 536 lost time injuries and 7813 working days lost. By 1988–89, among a staff of 1200, there were sixty-three lost time injuries and 641 working days lost. Manual handling was a big factor in loss time injury. Workers had to be trained to lift properly so they would not injure their backs. If a serious injury occurred, the safety officer had to notify the Workshops manager and the OHS Department, who would send an inspector. The safety officer would investigate, 'bring the community together to look at it' and discuss ways of avoiding a repeat of the circumstance. It is easy to see that, under such close scrutiny, dangerous initiation and prank practices that led to injuries could scarcely be passed off as industrial accidents. Even so, Mae Jean Parker experienced an initiation that included being suspended from a Workshops crane with a rod through the sleeves of her overalls, stretching her arms out in a cruciform position; she was also subjected to a number of other pranks, such as having the steel toe caps of her boots welded to the floor.

The technological changes at the Midland Railway Workshops from the 1960s to the 1990s had profound impacts on the trade structure, resulting in some trades declining or even ceasing to the practised, while new trades developed. These changes had equally profound impacts on the people who worked there; this will be shown even more to be the case in Chapter 7. The changes in the strengths and the nature of the trades and the adoption of a practice of accepting older apprentices with a higher educational standard for a shorter training period also altered the hierarchy and the craft consciousness of the Workshops. Undoubtedly, safer, more inclusive work practices empowered workers, making them more in control of their workplace and their health, but not of their long-term future, for within a decade of the adoption of the OHS legislation, the state government announced the Workshops' closure: the state's largest industrial workplace ceased operations one year later on 4 March 1994. A decade later, some workers still had difficulty accepting the closure.

7
Midland Railway Workshops: A history lesson?

'The lessons of history' may be a somewhat overworked phrase, as are dire warnings about what happens to those who don't learn from history. Nevertheless, this, like most sayings, holds a grain of truth. This chapter considers the value of learning from the fate of large industrial sites, and the historical significance of the Midland Railway Workshops in helping to tell that story. The impact of closure upon the economy, the transport and – most of all – the employees themselves ought not be forgotten. That impact could be interpreted for perpetuity if a portion of the Workshops site was set aside for the purpose of retaining the history and heritage, but it seems that – even more than the rest of the proud history– this is an aspect that the planners prefer to forget. This chapter sets the Workshops in the wider context of the fate of the state's rail industry. It will first discuss what happened, and then, how this should be remembered.

Elsewhere, I have argued that the closure of government industries and the selling off of government-run services to private companies is closely related to the shrinkage in union density and membership numbers in the unions remaining. The resultant changes in the rail transport industry, doubly hit by the switch to road transport and the privatisation of the government network, began in the early post World War II years.

In 1946, the Locomotive Engine Drivers', Firemen's and Cleaners' Union (LED), Western Australian division was involved in a lengthy and damaging strike over the issue of the safety of Australian Standard Garratt (ASG) locomotives. These two events, the strike and the closure, separated by half a century, stand at the beginning and end of a process that saw road transport taking over many of the functions previously undertaken by rail, and the government-owned rail network being prepared for privatisation. Government and private industry both claimed that these changes were essential to the modernisation and efficiency of the state's freight and transport systems, but for many of the workers involved they came at a high price.

How and why did these changes happen? Would studying the recent industrial history of Western Australia (and other places) have resulted in any different solutions? Could 'inevitable' changes have been handled better and managed more efficiently? A study of the state's industrial history reveals a complex story and provides some warnings for future transport planning when it comes to managing the fate of workers and their families.

How did it happen?

In September 1945, within weeks of World War II ending, the LED asked for a number of ASG locomotive engines to be withdrawn from service until an independent inquiry had been held on their safety. The ASGs were large, powerful, articulated engines, designed by Fred Mills, CME of the Midland Railway Workshops, for wartime conditions when Australia's railways urgently required heavy freight engines capable of running on the narrow-gauge, light railway lines in states such as Western Australia and Queensland. Although based on the original Garratt design by Beyer Peacock in Manchester, the ASGs, which were constructed in extreme haste, incorporated a number of cost-cutting measures. Originally leased to the states, the federal government offered the ASGs for purchase in 1944; altogether the WAGR bought twenty-five engines. By the end of the war, there had been many incidents of ASG derailment; one fatal accident was blamed on the extra width of the cabin. As well, crews had refused to take the engines through the low clearance Swan View Tunnel because of the danger of asphyxiation. The engines were difficult to work running in reverse and were unsuitable for shunting because on winter mornings excessive steam blows obscured visibility. They also took more time than other engines to be repaired in the Workshops, even though they were the newest locomotives in stock.

The minister for Railways in Frank Wise's Labor government, William Marshall, objected to the LED's request to withdraw the engines. Marshall stated that the 'colossal' sum of money spent on purchasing the engines and the lack of haulage power if they were taken off the road (which, he said, 'would provide an opportunity for road competition to become firmly established') made the union's request a 'very serious matter'. While Marshall's statement might have been regarded as an excuse for inaction, it shows that railway management was already aware that road transport might one day usurp rail as the major freight haulier.

Seeking to avert a major industrial dispute, Premier Wise persuaded the LED to continue working the engines while he appointed a Royal Commission into the ASGs. The Royal Commission met for six months, took evidence from numerous witnesses, including union members, and concluded in May 1946. Although the Royal Commissioner, Mr Justice Wolff, criticised the government for purchasing experimental engines, and recommended some forty repairs or alterations, he insisted that the engines be returned to service as soon as possible. Of most relevance to this discussion was the Royal Commissioner's conclusion that

> If the railways are to survive in a world of keen competition; if they are to fulfil their purpose in coordination with other forms of transport, they must be modernised. That means bigger and better locomotives. The policy of 'making do' (an expensive one, which has immediate and secondary effects) must be cast aside... Economic measures such as Transport Acts are of little use if they merely protect the Railways from competition. The Railways must be able to compete. If the Railways are unable to give service there will be a natural economic adjustment, perhaps slow, but nevertheless inexorable, in which the Railways will go down.

While accepting some of the Royal Commissioner's recommendations, the LED declared seven ASGs black and directed its members not to work on them. The matter went to the Arbitration Court, but no resolution was reached. The Arbitration Court president, Justice Dunphy, considered the union's ban unlawful. The Commissioner of Railways suspended six LED members who refused to work ASGs; the union demanded their reinstatement, and when this did not happen, went on strike from midnight on 6 November 1946. The Garratt strike, as it became known, involved not only the 1500 LED members, but also over 1000 Collie coal miners, who were stood down to avoid coal stockpiling. The strike created chaos in transport and communications, was disastrous economically for the state, and resulted in the union being deregistered from the Arbitration Court on 18 November, an action that caused widespread anger in the labour movement.

Settlement was reached on 22 November, with the government agreeing to undertake modifications recommended by an independent chairman before the engines could be returned to service, to support the LED's application to be reregistered and to drop legal proceedings against the strikers. Even so, the government remained condemned. In the 1947 election, many unions took their revenge by withholding funds from the ALP's campaign and some members even voted non-ALP. It was the state ALP's first election defeat since 1930. Despite the WAGR's insistence that the engines were safe and efficient, most of the ASGs were withdrawn from service by 1951 – a mere five years later. Significantly for the future, the Royal Commissioner's warning that the railways must be modernised to remain competitive was not heeded.

The Garratt strike was symptomatic of a number of union grievances in the early postwar years. The wave of militancy that swept WA unions in 1945 was spurred by the initial increase of the manufacturing workforce, and the strength of such unions as the AEU (one of the major unions at the Midland Railway Workshops), which increased its membership from a few hundred in the 1920s to 5000 in 1952. Many of these unions had communists on their executives, which impacted on the Midland Railway Workshops (see chapter 5). The militant unions expressed discontent with the moderate state ALP, as exemplified by the 1947 election result. These postwar changes facilitated the 1963 foundation of Western Australia's first independent trades and labour council (TLCWA) since the end of the nineteenth century. Until this time, the state ALP had organised politically and industrially, and unions had to be affiliated with the Party.

Just as the 1950s was the high point in the history of the Midland Railway Workshops, so, too, is that decade regarded as the heyday of the Australian union movement, during which union membership kept pace with the growth of the workforce. In 1953, 63 per cent of workers were unionised. By 1970 this had dropped to 49 per cent, but was again boosted in the early 1970s by the growth of the retail sector and other white-collar unions, the adoption of compulsory unionism agreements in some sectors and the growth of the power of the Australian Council of Trade Unions (ACTU), with Bob Hawke as president from 1969.

By 2001, however, only 25 per cent of Australian workers were unionised. This decline resulted from several factors: the reduction of the skilled trades workforce – a traditionally unionised (often closed shop) sector; the takeover of public sector industries, such as transport, by the private sector, where the closed shop was not observed; fewer full-time employees; and the increase in the number and proportion of jobs in sectors that were not traditionally unionised, such as tourism and hospitality. In 2004 only about 17 per cent of workers in the retail trade and 17.6 per cent of the cultural and recreational services sector were unionised. Two examples of the reduction of Western Australia's skilled trades workforce were the decline in membership of the LED and the closure of the state's biggest industrial factory and closed shop, the Midland Railway Workshops. In 1988, the LED secretary reported that his union's membership had dropped to 760, half what it was in 1946. He wrote:

> Decline due to dieselisation, the introduction of larger standard and narrow-gauge wagons and the elimination of single wagons, the closure of country lines and technology, the Government policy of modernisation and deregulation has led to reduced staff levels and lost work practices. Permanency is now a myth.

At the Railway Workshops, the workforce was reduced from 2300 in 1982 (including 500 apprentices) to 1094 in 1990, then 710 in 1992, with the Workshops finally closing in March 1994, a victim of the shift from state-owned industries to privatisation and from rail to road transport. The work went either to private companies or interstate. The workforce was impacted in many ways by the closure.

Why did it happen?

Why did the closure of the Workshops and the running down of the rail system happen? In short, latter twentieth century demands for modernisation and greater efficiency together with the economic rationalist belief that only private enterprise could deliver them brought inevitable changes. Public facilities began to be privatised and increasingly road haulage was favoured over rail transport. These changes were bound to impact disastrously on a government rail system and its many thousands of workers. This is starkly illustrated by a graph showing Westrail employee numbers (including Workshops employees) dropping from more than 9000 in 1981 to fewer than 2000 1998. Some, including members of parliament across the political spectrum, argued that the age of large industrial workshops was gone by the 1990s, and so it was inevitable – and indeed a sign of progress – that the Workshops and other government enterprises would close. Around Australia, other public facilities, including railway workshops at Eveleigh, Launceston and Ipswich, also closed during this period.

While the shift to privatisation and a growing hostility to trade unionism have often been dated from the era of economic rationalism, which commenced in the 1980s, it was arguably ushered in by the mineral boom in the northwest that began in the 1960s. Transnational companies with headquarters overseas, entering partnerships with major Australian-owned or operated companies such as Broken Hill Proprietary Limited (BHP) or Western Mining Corporation, brought with them a culture that was hostile to unions and a work ethic that broke down the established demarcations between one skilled trade and another, which previously had been safeguarded by the arbitration system. The problem of organising non-unionised workforces on mining sites occupied the TLCWA for much of its first decade. Its work yielded a period of union power in the 1970s and 1980s but by the end of the 1980s it was on the wane.

The privatisation debate in Australia was undoubtedly influenced by international events, especially the Thatcher government's early 1980s push to privatise many British public instrumentalities, including British Rail, and responses to Thatcherism by Australia's federal Labor government and the Liberal Party-led Opposition. The Hawke administration implemented the Prices and Incomes Accord, whereby unions promised industrial harmony in return for a system of wage indexation: the unions pledged not to demand wage rises in excess of the cost of living. The Accord (as it became known) was a divisive policy, especially among unions representing lower paid employees, but it was a powerful contributor to Labor's electoral success, as the previous government had been dogged by industrial turmoil, centred on wage rates. While the Accord was seen by many as a union taming instrument used by the ALP to make Labor a more attractive alternative to a new electorate with a declining blue-collar workforce, the unions stood to gain very little from the agreement. Indeed, the TLCWA found the state Labor administrations of Brian Burke and his successors quite unsympathetic in disputes with major transnational companies, such as Robe River Iron Ore and Peko Wallsend. In a climate in which both sides of politics increasingly adopted Thatcherite policies of economic rationalism, Australian state and federal Labor governments appeared keener on providing efficient and acquiescent workforces than remaining true to their roots in upholding workers' rights.

In Western Australia, the Burke Government and the TLCWA had come to an agreement similar to the Accord, made official by the *WA Labor Tripartite Consultative Council Act*, 1983. The tripartite (government, industry, unions) negotiations included a rewriting of the obsolete *Industrial Arbitration Act* and the establishment of an Occupational Health and Safety Commission, both much needed. But as had the federal Accord, the Tripartite Council drew criticism because it effectively muzzled opposition from the unions. The government proceeded with unpopular civil service retrenchments, including the loss of 323 jobs when the Public Works Department Architectural Division ceased operations in September 1984, and restructured or sold off state instrumentalities and assets without consulting the union movement and, with the tacit support of the TLC. Burke's rationale for implementing these harsh measures was a $274 million shortfall in the budget, which his administration had inherited from the previous government. By the end of 1985, many unions had come to believe that the privatisation of the public sector and the deregulation of the labour market was state government policy.

Responses to privatisation

Over a period of several months, commencing in December 1985, the TLCWA launched three anti-privatisation campaigns that aimed to educate the public on the probable effects of government privatising the public sector and deregulating the labour market. The TLCWA invited David Heald to visit Western Australia. Heald was an economist from the University of Glasgow, who the ACTU hired as a consultant to research privatisation and the erosion of the public sector. In a report for the ACTU, Heald drew some 'disturbing parallels between the United Kingdom in 1976 and Australia in 1986', including financial problems, an agreement between government and unions, public hostility to trade unions, and a New Right Opposition that had seized the policy initiative'. But Heald placed the Australian labour movement in a much stronger position to resist the encroachment of New Right economics. He pointed to the fact that the discipline shown by trade unions resulted in a far more effective Accord than the Social Contract between the Labour Party and British unions, which culminated in a wages explosion in 1976. Heald argued that, after several years of Thatcher government, the New Right agenda could hardly be held up as a fresh approach by Australian Liberals; its problems, including massive unemployment and 'territorial, social and racial divisions', were obvious to everyone. Also, the federal system militated against the centralising of power enacted by the Thatcher government, as state and territory governments jealously guarded their powers. Lastly, Heald believed that John Howard appeared 'to lack the personal stature necessary to project himself as an alternative prime minister' and that he was 'clearly unsure of where to position himself given the rightward drift of the Federal Labor Government and the emergence of an aggressive New Right outside Parliament'. Subsequent history would prove Heald wrong on several counts.

Heald's report showed unions the need for coordination between their state and federal bodies, and an increased emphasis on convincing public sector employers of the 'wisdom of using public sector employment rather than transferring the work to the private sector'. The TLCWA launched the second, and later a third stage of their anti-privatisation campaign in 1987, and the state ALP gave in principle support to its opposition to the federal move to privatise public assets. The federal ALP's position had changed rapidly by June 1988, when plans to sell off Qantas, Trans Australian Airlines and the Commonwealth Bank emerged. Even the state ALP's commitment to public assets was changing, with Premier Peter Dowding stating:

> Much of the debate on public enterprise seems to be centred on the ownership question, *whereas it should be focused on the performance and efficiency of their operations.* The Government takes pride in its performance in these two critical areas – a performance which has increased the security, and enhanced the quality of employment in the public sector. Hence, whilst we will be continuing efforts to improve efficiency, there are no current plans to pursue the issue of privatisation (my emphasis).

The complexities of the issue were increased by the fact that while most public sector unions, whose membership would be most impacted by the move to privatise public assets, strongly opposed privatisation, some other unions showed stolid indifference to attempts to raise their members' awareness.

In March 1989, Bob Hawke's favourable reaction to Liberal Party plans to privatise many government authorities if they should gain government angered the TLCWA. Assistant Secretary Rob Meecham reminded the prime minister of the ACTU's support for 'full public ownership and control of existing enterprises at the Federal, State and Local level' and reiterated that the TLCWA would fight 'the privatisation of these authorities ... fiercely and with all the reserves available to it'. In July 1989, TLCWA State Secretary Clive Brown addressed a meeting of TLC members and representatives of the state Liberal Party on privatisation. He concluded that there was an 'overwhelming argument for [a] strong and viable public sector for strategic and service grounds'. Leader of the Opposition Richard Court responded that the Liberals were opposed to government involvement in the private sector. But the Party believed there was a 'limited role for government, for example within a mixed public and private power industry'. This position was to have great significance for the Midland Railway Workshops when Court's Liberal Party was elected to government early in 1993.

The Liberal Party's only other response to the issue of privatisation was to send the ALP a copy of a paper produced by the Australian Society of Accountants, entitled 'Long Road to Reform: Privatisation and Corporatisation in Australia'. This paper extensively quoted Kenneth Wiltshire, Professor of Public Administration at Queensland University, who claimed that the Hawke government mishandled its attempts to privatise public enterprises by 'giving Australian unions and their factional allies within the ALP time to mobilise'. Consequently, a 'grand plan of assets sales' soon deteriorated into 'a highly publicised saga of reversals, relaunches, inventions of new terminology and recycled options'. Wiltshire claimed that some of these policy reversals could be explained purely and simply by 'loyalty to the traditions of the institutions themselves, many of which were formed by Labor governments'. He claimed that 'reluctance to step away from the original social [goals] rather than the business goals of many government enterprises' made the Labor government very vulnerable to the union movement, which was lobbying against change. The result was that the Left factions of the ALP, aided by a well-researched and articulate ACTU campaign, succeeded in blocking each attempt by the Hawke government to move the privatisation process forward. Wiltshire saw the situation as stalled rather than collapsed. Subsequent events proved the accuracy of his analysis.

The anti-privatisation lobby should have been warned by the paper's

Protests to save the Workshops took various forms including street marches and an attempt to drag a damaged diesel locomotive back from Forrestfield to the Workshops. (Photo courtesy of Barry Watts)

concluding paragraph. The authors suggested that the Liberal Party should begin asking some hard questions, for example: 'Why does the government own Australian Airlines? Why should universities be run from Canberra [that is, by the Federal Government]? How did Telecom Australia get its telecommunications monopoly in the first place?' The thirteen page paper concluded that questions such as these

> would have seemed absurd to a previous generation, which was more concerned to see that Australia got the infrastructure it needed than to quibble much about how it was run, in whose interests it was run and which particular groups were at the wrong end of the cross-subsidies. Now, questions like this do not seem at all silly. This is why the debate over corporatisation and privatisation is going to have its day again.

What would aid this circumstance? By the mid 1990s, Labor governments had been voted out of office federally and in every

Australian state and territory except New South Wales. Their successful political opponents espoused and legislated economic rationalist policies, unfettered by any alliance with trade unions or, it would appear, any loyalty to wage earners. In 1993 in Western Australia, the Liberal–National Party coalition, led by Richard Court, took office. Within weeks, the government had revealed that it would close the Midland Railway Workshops and the Robb Jetty Meat Works. It also announced staff cuts in other government instrumentalities, such as BankWest, the State Government Insurance Commission and the State Electricity Commission. The government then embarked on a series of reforms that would dismantle the industrial relations system that had served Western Australia for most of the twentieth century. The Court government's legislation brought the state to a standstill with massive protests and Days of Action, yet it served as a model for the industrial relations policy initiated by the Howard administration after its federal election victory in 1996. Privatisation and individual workplace agreements formed the centrepiece of this policy.

Impacts on the Workshops workforce

In 2004, a decade after the closure, Peter Carty, a former boilermaker, was among dozens of past employees interviewed by the Midland Railway Workshops History Project. Standing in his former workplace, the deserted and gutted boiler shop, Carty looked into the camera lens. 'I stand here and tell you, I served my time with a guy – I won't mention his name …' He cleared his throat and looked away before saying that the man committed suicide. 'We were shattered.' Speaking of the closure of the 1994 Midland Workshops, Carty narrowed his eyes, reliving the moment. 'I was angry … angry … very angry.' Elsewhere, and at greater length, Carty recounted the closure:

> They sacked all these bloody people … They [didn't] debrief you. If you've been trained up to that and you're good at what you're doing [and] they don't debrief you, meaning that, okay, this is going to happen and that's going happen. All those clever bastards, you know. How do you tell thousands of blokes that? They just shut the gate. 'There you go. Bad luck.' … Some blokes never got a job again – never got a job again – never ever – and can't understand why they could never get a job again because they had always worked. Lined up, did their job faithfully. 'I never did anything wrong' [was their reaction] … One particular bloke, I grew up

> with him [and] he gives me his money and says, 'You're a grandfather' and he went home and shot himself. Some blokes drunk [sic] themselves to death. Other blokes went home and beat their kids and all sorts of things because it was so – 'What do I do?'. It was like coming out of the army or an army area now. They weren't debriefed. If they shut a place down now, they start to farm you out easy if you've been a position a long time. They didn't do that.

Sindy Hunter 'felt angry for years because the government stole my whole choice of life off me'. She found that as a qualified but inexperienced mechanical fitter she could not get a job in a private firm. Robert Rowe, a former foreman, spoke of the Workshops as a 'family thing, [a place where] generations of people found work' and were trained for a trade. Words such as 'surreal', 'sad' and 'broken promises' – the latter referring to the Liberal–National Party Coalition state administration of Premier Richard Court (1993–2001), which had promised to upgrade the Workshops if elected – were used to describe often angry feelings and reactions. These reactions were not limited to blue-collar staff. Timekeeper Kevin Mountain, who had worked for forty-two years at the Workshops, went home and waited for a telephone call, telling him that it was all a mistake and he could have his job back. Reflecting on his experience a decade later he felt that he should have received trauma counselling.

At the televised announcement of the closure, Transport Minister Eric Charlton promised that workers would be relocated and would not lose their jobs. But what did he actually mean? A printout of redundancies, transfers and redeployment of staff at the Workshops at the date of closure indicates that, out of 324 employees, 182 accepted redundancy, 138 were transferred to other Westrail divisions, two were redeployed, one retired and one was listed as deceased. This may have been the man to whom Peter Carty referred. Undoubtedly, some of the redundancy payouts helped younger employees set up their own businesses, but transfers masks demotion. In her study of the impact of the closure, historian Lyla Elliott found that those who were offered jobs often found themselves placed in menial tasks that belied their skills and experience. Elliott cited the case of a crankshaft grinder operator – a job that required making exact judgements 'within a thousandths of an inch' – who was redeployed cleaning carriages, and another of a wagon inspector who was offered temporary work digging holes for telephone cables. Not surprisingly, some highly skilled tradesmen chose redundancy rather than accept lower paid, soul-destroying work. But they could not escape the depression that often followed when men who had worked all their lives felt unwanted and thrown on the scrap heap. There were success stories. Several men set up their own businesses, and some found similar skilled employment in private sector firms that were taking on Westrail work, but these were in the minority. Most of the men who Elliott interviewed agreed that those few who were successful were largely middle to top management, white-collar workers and some tradespeople.

This is perhaps not so surprising given the types of services made available to staff in preparation for the Workshops' closure, which consisted mostly of small business and financial planning seminars, and a two-day workshop by the Career Development Centre on topics that included how to handle stress, which was offered in the latter part of 1993. The need for a change management program was identified by those tasked with preparing staff for the closure. The statements in one circular alone should have warned management that there were going to be significant problems.

> Unacceptably high levels of stress are being experienced by large numbers of employees at the Midland site. The number of people absent from work due to stress related illness is steadily increasing.
>
> Employees are not demonstrating that they are able to identify their transferable skills and competencies, though extensive competency audits have been carried out on a number of the job clusters at the Midland site.
>
> Resistance to change is widespread because individuals are
> – in denial
> – fear the loss of work social group
> – identifying themselves with their current job
> – doubt their capacity to perform other types of work.

The Career Development Centre's workshop appears to have been devised to meet these challenges. It catered for a maximum of twenty participants and cost $500 per day, a cost presumably met by Westrail. Whether more than one of these workshops was organised is unknown, but perhaps most important is the perception by many former employees that no assistance was available to enable them to transition to post-Workshops life. Although the impact that redundancy or demotion has upon workers was better understood a decade later when most of these men were reflecting upon their experience, it seems evident that, even by the standards of the day, the changed management process was not well handled. Some workers were given assistance to prepare for life after the Workshops, but they were comparatively few.

Long-term impacts

What have been the long-term impacts of the Workshops' closure on the economy and on workers? Clearly, as private industry has not taken the place of major state-owned enterprises, a major effect has been the reduction of opportunities for training skilled workers. That the ongoing skills shortage is a significant issue for twenty-first century Australia is evidenced by the amount of media coverage that this topic has attracted in recent years. A 2005 survey indicated that the skills shortage was blamed for retarding industrial development and for causing accidents, and had inspired numerous solutions, including the contentious short-term visas for immigrant workers. Yet few of the proposed solutions take more than a cursory glimpse at the historical background of apprenticeship training in Australia. It seems that governments and employers are very reluctant to learn from history.

Apart from the immediate effects on Workshops employees, closures and sell-offs related to privatisation had massive effects across the state's (and Australia's) rail systems. During the 1980s and 1990s, there were staffing cuts and redundancies among train crews. Inevitably, job losses led to a decline in union membership, which removed protection from workers, especially with regard to workplace safety, working conditions and unfair dismissal.

Massive redundancies occurred across state rail networks from 1993. The Rail, Tram and Bus Union (RTBU), which the LED amalgamated with in 1999, summarised the national situation after several years of Howard government policies:

> First there were waves of voluntary redundancies as modern technology, competitive tendering and privatisation programs caught up with what was an under-invested, steam-era industry ... The traditional railway Workshops was rapidly modernised in Queensland, South Australia and Tasmania, with considerable job losses. The Workshops was closed or privatised in Western Australia and New South Wales, and with the sale of Australian National Railways in late 1997, the South Australian railway

Workshops was sold and savagely cut. To fight these trends, the RTBU put forward detailed industry policy initiatives, which the Keating Labor government spurned, and the Howard Coalition government never even considered. The Keating Labor government offered Labour Adjustment Programs to help retrain redundant railway workers, but the Howard Coalition government only offers unemployment benefits and the very limited training available through the Jobs Network. The RTBU supports training and labour market programs, too, but these are not enough to reduce unemployment and to create efficient industries.

The RTBU claimed that when the US rail company Wisconsin Central Transportation purchased the privatised Australian Southern Railroad in 1997, 50 per cent of jobs were lost. The union stated that Wisconsin Central and the British company Serco (owner of three of Australia's most famous rail routes, the Indian Pacific, The Ghan and The Overland) forced workers to sign individual contracts (Australian Workplace Agreements, known as AWAs) if they wanted to keep their jobs, irrespective of the employees' repeated desire to have the RTBU negotiate an enterprise agreement with the new employers. Under the AWAs the union's power to represent workers was limited to health and safety issues. In South Australia and Tasmania, the workers won back their right to collective bargaining only after protracted court battles.

The present-day RTBU is an amalgamation of three former railway unions, including the LED, and a bus and tram workers union. While a relatively small union in Western Australia, the RTBU claims an Australia-wide membership of 35,000 in the transport industry (5000 more than the figures provided in 2009), but this covers all forms of private and public road and rail transport. There is also the much larger Transport Workers Union of Australia, with a national membership of around 90,000 workers in aviation, oil, waste management, gas, road transport, passenger vehicles and freight logistics. The overwhelming majority of these members work in the public sector. In 2004, when union density in the public sector still stood at 46.4 per cent, it was at a low 17.4 per cent in the private sector. The presence of unions, of course, did not save the Midland Railway Workshops – and some would argue that the union activity was what made the Workshops particularly vulnerable to New Right ideology.

While the decline in union membership and density can be clearly traced through statistics, the extent of the emotional cost for redundant workers – in broken lives, spirits, relationships and marriages – is far harder to assess. Are the ex-Midland Workshops employees correct in saying that today, the experience of workers made redundant would be better than it was in 1994? Recent closures of works elsewhere in Australia seem to suggest not. If so, this makes the experiences of the Midland Workshops employees all the more poignant and important to preserve. While solutions do not lie in the past, it is only in researching the circumstances of past history and the impact of particular outcomes on individual lives that we can hope to avoid repeating the same mistakes and recreating the same cycles of misery.

The Midland Railway Workshops buildings remain a physical reminder of Western Australia's largest industrial endeavour in the twentieth century. Somewhere in these buildings, decency dictates, there must be space to tell the whole story of what happened here, including what happened to those workers whose lives were irrevocably changed and, in some cases, destroyed by their closure.

8
What Now?

The 4 March 2019 marks the twenty-fifth anniversary of the Midland Railway Workshops' closure. In the quarter of a century that has passed, what has happened to the site? In 2000, the Court government appointed the MRA to a fifteen-year tenure to redevelop the site. The MRA's agenda was to demolish the buildings and construct new ones. They began by removing the Shell Annexe to make way for a road to the new police complex at the eastern end of the site. Fortunately, a change of government in 2001 resulted in the site being declared a heritage icon in 2004, which meant that the significant buildings (the three main blocks, the CME's office, the foundry, the power house, the pattern shop, the Railway Institute building and the timekeeper's office) were saved from demolition. Yet, to walk around the site late in 2018 was to walk in a ghost town.

One could argue that much has been done with this huge and problematic site. Pollutants, including soil contamination and asbestos roofing, were removed and replaced. The peace memorial has been refurbished and made accessible to the public for Anzac Day and other ceremonies. Land west of the Coal Dam is now a housing estate, roads have been created and named and a small portion of the main buildings has been converted to other uses. Because no major developer was prepared to take over and redevelop the site, however, the question arises as to whether development will be piecemeal and whether one type of development is compatible with another.

Block 1 is the only one of the main blocks to retain railway lines and inspection pits. It was the ideal site for a rail heritage centre complete with engines and rolling stock. Yet this is the only block to have had any appreciable conversion to new use. The eastern-most quarter of Block 1 houses a medical superclinic, a building within a building that does not impact upon the external appearance of this heritage-listed site. The remaining three-quarters of the building (now fenced off) remains a wasteland of empty floor and drifting leaves. This section still contains the railway lines and inspection pits so it could be used to house engines and carriages. But would this use be compatible with the clinic?

Around the site is further evidence of a lack of planning. An incongruous and irrelevant mural, looking like a scene from a Dickensian novel, decorates one wall. While the streets, lanes and other features in the main part of the site were given generic names, referencing their Workshops past, such as Main Gate, Woodmill Lane and Foundry Road, those in the vicinity of the Coal Dam have been named after collieries in Collie, the origin of most of the coal used by WAGR–Westrail: Wyvern, Wallsend, Griffin, Stockton, Centaur and Cardiff. These names have minimal relevance to the site and, in the workers' eyes, would more than anything else, frequently have been connected with bosses and unfair work practices. If origins was intended to be a theme for naming or renaming, why wasn't the place that is now called Railway Square not named for its original use – the Shunting Yard?

No person connected with the Workshops is commemorated in site names, except that of the engineer, Charles Yelverton O'Connor, whose second given name was used in the renaming of Montreal Road East. Despite the folklore that credits O'Connor with building the Workshops, his role did not extend much beyond selecting the site and submitting the first plan. Thomas Rotherham, O'Connor's successor, was the real architect of the Workshops, but most people have never heard his name. Then there were the CMEs and masters of apprentices, whose decisions impacted workers on a daily basis. Why not Broadfoot Way, Groves Lane or Kirkham Road? John Broadfoot was works manager, and then CME of the Workshops; George Groves and Bill Kirkham were both masters of apprentices. Last, and most importantly, the workers themselves and especially the shop stewards dedicated to improving conditions in a dangerous workplace, including the legendary Jack Marks, should be honoured.

Was the public consulted about how names would be chosen? The MetRA's 2017 *Heritage Interpretation Strategy* states that 'All of the community is encouraged to undertake interpretation when the opportunity arises as all sectors have a role to play in keeping alive

Incongruous and irrelevant. This mural does not depict Workshops life or activity. (Photo courtesy of Bobbie Oliver)

the stories of Midland in both private development sites and in public areas'. What better opportunity for community involvement could there have been than a competition to name streets on the site?

Much is at stake here. The Midland Railway Workshops site could become a model for the creative interpretation and reuse of major industrial sites. This has not happened so far and as the years since the closure lengthen, despite the extensive archive of documents, photographs and artefacts collected by the Midland Workshops History Project, and the papers, chapters and books that have been published, the history is not being retained on the site. Perhaps this is because the objects and products of research are dispersed. Bringing together a number of revised papers in one book is my attempt to gather some of the research into one place and to remind stakeholders and others of what could be achieved at the site. This aim would be greatly enhanced by funded permanent display areas, rather than

The Workers Wall is a demonstration of creative artwork that is relevant to the site. (Above) Bricks with individual workers' names and the jobs they held in the Workshops. (Opp.) An example of original Workshops art: Caricatures of Workshops' employees by Ray Montgomery. (Wall photo courtesy of Bobbie Oliver; Art photo courtesy of Workshops History Project)

leaving it up to the individual developer to decide whether any form of interpretation is worthwhile.

This latter approach is evident throughout the MetRA's *Heritage Interpretation Strategy*. In the Introduction, the reader is advised that 'The Strategy is not a statutory document; it offers guidance but is not prescriptive'. Furthermore, 'Whilst the themes, messages and storylines in the Strategy provide guidance, developers may propose alternative interpretation'. This begs the question: What would alternative interpretation look like? How accurate would it be? Even less prescriptive is the statement that, 'It is *hoped* (my emphasis) that developers and individuals will take the opportunity to acknowledge and celebrate the history of Midland through interpretation initiatives even when it's

not a requirement of development approval'. This statement also begs an obvious question as to why interpretation isn't a requirement of all development approval on a site that has been declared a state heritage icon. Further, what incentives are being offered for developers to yield space and resources to interpretation? What access do they have to the historical collections and published research produced by the History Project? Do they know anything about the history or the historiography of the site? Would they know how to interpret it if they did have access to this material? This type of work requires skilled interpreters: historians, museum curators and other heritage professionals. It is not an ability that is just picked up. Millions of dollars have been expended on this site and yet there are no resources to ensure that any developer receives professional assistance for interpretation that should be mandatory upon any heritage site development.

The *Heritage Interpretation Strategy* also states that, 'A 2016 initiative to reopen the Time Keeper's Office as a café and interpretive hub is being pursued'. Yet in June 2018, the building remained empty and a 'For Lease' sign was up outside it. The *Strategy* also mentions open days on the site. The last open day was held in 2013.

None of these criticisms are meant to suggest that there is no value in the *Heritage Interpretation Strategy*. There are some very relevant ideas, such as the installation of graphic panels and projections. There is so much photographic material available as subjects for artwork and creative photographic displays. The use of photographs on the blinds installed on the Interpretive Centre is an excellent example.

The Workers' Wall, encompassing bricks bearing the names of former workers, is another example of how attractive artwork might convey historical meaning. But these initiatives preceded the MetRA. More recent site decorations, such as the previously mentioned mural and the luridly lit Tower of Memory convey absolutely nothing of significance or meaning and have no connection with the former Workshops.

What sort of heritage centre or museum?

Somewhere in these buildings there must be space to tell the whole story of what happened here, including what happened to those workers whose lives were irrevocably changed and, in some cases, destroyed by their closure. Perhaps this statement suggests, in transport historian Colin Divall's words, 'that exhibitions really change the way people understand [the] past', an assumption he believed was debatable at best. What sort of exhibitions would not merely attract a modern public – for many of whom rail travel is limited to suburban transport, if indeed they travel by rail at all – but also encourage it to learn new things about the past and question commonly held beliefs?

In a paper written in 2008, Divall provided some helpful guidelines about the forms that such exhibitions might take. First, he stated that 'getting visitors to recognise that there can be more than one way to view the past *and* that it is possible to weigh these [ways], however provisionally, in the balance is more important than trying to 'sell' them any particular account'. In other words, it's better to present two alternative versions of history and let people work out for themselves which they think is the more acceptable than to tell people what to think. The previous chapters have given numerous instances of the richness and variety of stories from the Midland Railway Workshops that can be presented from more than one perspective: bosses versus workers in the natural battleground, workers who loved the factory environment, workers who hated every minute that they spent there, the Workshops closed because they were outdated and unproductive *or* to meet an economic rationalist and union-busting agenda, the initiations – harmless fun, useful lessons or dangerous bullying? There are many more.

Second, Divall mentioned ways of presenting railways 'as symbols of [national] identity'. There is considerable evidence to develop themes along these lines. The railway infrastructure was the biggest investment that many Australian colonial governments made and they did so in order to open up and exploit the inland. Australia may have ridden on the sheep's back, but it was the railways that made this possible by transporting wool (and wheat) from the places of production to the ports and markets. Development was aided and hindered by decisions about the types of gauge chosen by the different colonies, with Western Australia and Queensland opting for narrow gauge railways, while the other colonies chose standard or broad gauge. For many years, the adoption of standard gauge lines around Australia was regarded as the solution to a problem that required passengers and freight to change trains at every border. Ironically, for Western Australia, the introduction of standard gauge lines ultimately enabled the National Rail Corporation to take over much of the rail system, employing crews from the eastern states to bring trains right through to Kwinana and cutting out local crews.

With regard to another determinant of national identity – Australia's involvement in overseas wars – there is plenty of material, too. The previously mentioned honour boards detail the sacrifice of Workshops employees who served in World War I, listing the dead the returned men. Some Workshops employees served in railway regiments on the Western Front. Much research remains to be done on this type of war service. Conversely, during World War II, many railway employees were barred from military service because they were deemed to be in an industry essential to the war effort. And indeed, part of the war effort was made here at Midland in the forms of munitions, repairs for US Navy submarines and the design and building of that notorious wartime locomotive, the Australian Standard Garratt. Many of these stories still await telling.

Divall also advocated using 'media, which many people find attractive [such as] film, prints, posters, photographs, cartoons [and] drama'. The Midland History Project collected masses of such material, some of which was displayed in the Interpretive Centre from 2005 to 2008. As well as the audio and video material of workers describing their Workshops lives and their feelings about the closure, there are also photographs from throughout the entire history, ranging from private snapshots to official site photographs, some dating from as early as 1910, brochures and promotional films, news footage of the closure announcement, artwork, including cartoons of individual workers drawn by employee Ray Montgomery, who was a talented artist, models of the site, poetry and memoirs. Many of these items are held in collections in the State Library of Western Australia and the Midland Local History Library. They are merely waiting for a place to be displayed. But with a merger of MetRA with Landcorp already in process and scheduled to be completed by 2019, any predictions about what this means for the Midland Workshops site would be speculatory.

ENDNOTES

Introduction

p. 1. Ron Wadham is quoted from his unpublished memoir, 'Ronald Arthur Wadham with the WAGR 1969 to 1989', donated to Midland Workshops History Project Collection, State Library of Western Australia (SLWA) Acc. no. 7625A/22/ Wadham, n.d., Supplement 2, 'Industrial Relations', 1.

Chapter 1

The chapter's title and the quote on p. 4 are from Bernard Carney, 'The Midland Railway Workshops', *West*, CD (2002).

p. 5. Regarding the 're-interpretation' of East Perth, see Jenny Gregory, 'Obliterating History? The Transformation of Inner City Industrial Suburbs', *Australian Historical Studies*, 39 (2008): 91–106. The version of the *Burra Charter* cited here and elsewhere is Marquis-Kyle, Peter and Walker, Meredith, *The Illustrated Burra Charter*, (Sydney: ICOMOS, 1992).

p. 6. Graeme Aplin is cited from *Heritage. Identification, Conservation and Management* (South Melbourne: Oxford University Press, 2002), 7–10.

p. 6-8. For information on Midland and the Workshops, see *The Workshops. A history of the Midland Government Railway Workshops*, ed. Patrick Bertola and Bobbie Oliver (Nedlands: UWA Press, 2006). Cited here are Ann Highfield, 'Midland, the suburb', 39–60; Philippa Rogers 'The Workshops – the heart of the railway system' (especially 37); see also, Linley Batterham, 'Women munitions workers, 1943–45', in *ibid*, 128–43; Bobbie Oliver, 'The Apprenticeship System at the Workshops' in *ibid*, 66–67; Charlie Fox, 'Work Organisation', in *ibid*, 81–105; Lyla Elliott, "Derailed': The closure of the Midland Workshops', in *ibid*, 235–58. These chapters, and others from *The Workshops* are quoted throughout this book.

p. 8-9. Information on the heritage assessments and significance of the site is from Heritage and Conservation Professionals, 'Draft Heritage Strategy for Midland Central Redevelopment Area, prepared for the Midland Redevelopment Authority, Strategy Paper no. 1', (2001), (referred to in the text as the 'Strategy Paper'). For open days, see Midland Redevelopment Authority, *The First Five Years 2000–2005*, accessed on 17 July 2018 at cdn.mra.wa.gov.au/production/documents-media/documents/midland/file/the-first-five-years-2000-2005.pdf.

p. 10. The six industry partners in the first grant (2000–01) were the Australian Society for the Study of Labour History, Perth Branch (the Labour History Society), the J. S. Battye Library of Western Australian History (Battye Library) and the Western Australian branches of four trade unions: the Communications, Electrical, Engineering and Plumbing Union (CEPU), the Australian Manufacturing Workers Union (AMWU), the Australian Services Union (ASU) and the Rail, Tram and Bus Industry Union (RTBU). To these were added (2002–04) the State Record Office of Western Australia (SROWA), the Museum of Western Australia, Unions WA, the Midland Redevelopment Authority (MRA) and the City of Swan.

p. 11. Peter Spearritt, 'Money, Taste and Industrial Heritage', in *Packaging the Past? Public Histories*, ed. John Rickard and Peter Spearritt (Melbourne: Melbourne University Press, 1991), 33.

p. 14. A copy of Ric McCracken's paper, 'Planning for a State Rail Heritage Centre at the Midland Workshops' (2002) is held with other papers of the Midland Workshops History Project, SLWA Acc. no. 7625A/22/McCracken.

p. 15. Associate Professor Lucy Taksa's address was published in *Papers in Labour History*, no. 25, *The WAGR/Westrail Workshops* (September 2001), 101–16.

p. 15-16. Steven High and David W. Lewis, *Corporate Wasteland. The Landscape and Memory of Deindustrialisation* (New York: Cornell University Press, 2007), 29–30. The National Museum of Industrial History's website can be accessed at discoverlehighvalley.com/listing/national-museum-of-industrial-history/3385/

p. 20. The MRA's vision statement is from Midland Redevelopment Authority, *Concept Planning for State Railway Heritage Centre Tender Brief* (Midland: MRA, 2003), 2. The *Draft Concept Plan*, (Midland: MRA, 2000) is also cited. The three feasibility studies that the MRA commissioned were David Farr and Associates, *Feasibility Study* (2003); Sanmor and Associates (2006) at Sanmor and Associates Projects: Cultural Centres, sanmor.com.au/midland.html, and Forrest and Spiers (2008).

p. 22. The MRA and the MetRA are cited, respectively, from Midland Redevelopment Authority, 'Planning – Helena Precinct' (Midland: MRA, 2009), and Metropolitan Redevelopment Authority, *Midland Heritage Interpretation Strategy* (Perth, MetRA, 2017), Appendix 3, 'Midland Railway Workshops Interpretation'.

p. 23. Information about the STEAM Museum is from its webpage: STEAM Museum of the Great Western Railway, steam-museum.org.uk/aboutus/Pages/The-Displays.aspx. Oliver and Reeves are quoted from Bobbie Oliver and Andrew Reeves, 'Crossing Disciplinary Boundaries: Labour History and Museum Studies', in *Labour History*, no. 85 (November 2003), 5.

Chapter 2

p. 27. For information on Thomas Rotherham and the building of the Workshops, see Richard G. Hartley, 'Midland Junction Workshops: Mechanical engineering and Government policies', in *The Workshops*, 106–27.

p. 29-30. Neil McDougall is quoted from his interview with Bonnie Mitchell, 2003, SLWA Accession no. OH3443. The information about accidents and fatalities is from *Chief Mechanical Engineer's Annual Reports* (1957), 22 and (1967), 24, and a table compiled from these reports (1903–73) by my researcher, Linley Batterham. Peter Carty was interviewed by Mia Lindgren on 'Everyday Life', *Midland Workshops Life*, directed and produced by Mia Lindgren, DVD (Murdoch: Murdoch University, 2004).

p. 31. Patrick Gayton, interviewed by Kendall Crake, 20 March 2003, SLWA Acc. no. OH3429. Peter Carty, interviewed by Chelsea Gellard, 9 May 2002, SLWA Acc. no. OH 3251.

Chapter 3

p. 36-7 . E. J. Hobsbawm is quoted from 'Trade Union History', *Economic History Review* 20, no. 2 (August 1967), 358 and 'The New Unionism Reconsidered' in *The Development of Trade Unionism in Great Britain and Germany, 1880–1914*, ed. W. J. Mommsen & H.-G. Husung (London: George Allen & Unwin, 1985), 13.

p. 38-9. Historical background is from Tom Sheridan, *Mindful Militants. The Amalgamated Engineering Union in Australia, 1920–1972* (Cambridge: Cambridge University Press, 1975), ix and 12, and Ian Turner, *Industrial Labour and Politics. The dynamics of the Labour movement in Eastern Australia 1900–1921* (Canberra: Australian National University Press, 1965), 7. For the ALP and the Trades and Labour Council in Western Australia, see Bobbie Oliver, *Unity is Strength. A history of the Australian Labor Party and the Trades and Labor Council in Western Australia* (Perth, API Books, 2003).

p. 39. For colonial labour in Western Australia, see Ian H. vanden Driesen, 'The Evolution of the Trade Union Movement in Western Australia', in *A New History of Western Australia*, ed. C. T. Stannage, (Nedlands: UWA Press, 1981),

35–80, and Joan Williams, *The First Furrow* (Willagee: Lone Hand Press, 1976). For Robert Hollis, see C. Docherty, 'Hollis, Robert (1851–1937)', *Australian Dictionary of Biography*, National Centre of Biography, Australian National University, published first in hardcopy 1983. For a history of the Locomotive Engine Drivers' Union see Bobbie Oliver, *The Locomotive Enginemen. A history of the West Australian Locomotive Engine Drivers', Firemen's and Cleaners Union*, (Perth: Black Swan Press, 2016).

p. 40-1. William Somerville is quoted from 'An Economic History of Western Australia, with Special Reference to Trade Unions and the Influence of the Industrial Court of Arbitration', unpublished manuscript, n.d., SLWA, Acc. no. 451A, vol. II, 346–47. For details of training and career structure, see Oliver, *The Locomotive Enginemen*; see also Transport Union Papers, SLWA MN 2472 Acc. no. 5256A, file 186, Promotion of Call Boys 1915–1951. Jack Emery is quoted from his memoir, 'Learning a trade: Memories of an Apprentice Turner and Iron Machinist, 29 January 1940 to 1 April 1945', *Papers in Labour History*, no. 25 (September 2001), 10.

p. 42. Stuart Macintyre, 'Basic Wage', in *The Oxford Companion to Australian History*, ed. Graeme Davison, John Hirst and Stuart Macintyre (Oxford: Oxford University Press, 1998), 62. Changes to the apprenticeship system are outlined in Minutes of the Industrial Training Advisory Council (ITAC), 8 April 1987, in WAGR Papers, SROWA Cons 5692, item 7140/87. For changes to the apprenticeship system in Britain since the 1970s, see, for example, A. L. Booth and S. E. Satchell, 'Apprenticeships and Job Tenure', *Oxford Economic Papers*, 46 (1994): 676–95; Jonathan Payne, 'The changing meaning of skill and its implications for UK vocational education and training policy'(1999), Eurofound: the European Foundation for the improvement of living and working conditions, accessed 24 September at eurofound.europa.eu/publications/article/1999/the-changing-meaning-of-skill-and-its-implications-for-uk-vocational-education-and-training-policy; Jonathan Payne, 'National Skills Task Force issues final report' (2000), Eurofound: the European Foundation for the improvement of living and working conditions, accessed 24 September at eurofound.europa.eu/publications/article/2000/national-skills-task-force-issues-final-report.
Jonathan Payne (2002), 'Government seeks to expand and revitalise modern apprenticeships', Eurofound: the European Foundation for the improvement of living and working conditions, accessed 24 September 2018 at eurofound.europa.eu/lv/publications/article/2002/government-seeks-to-expand-and-revitalise-modern-apprenticeships.

p. 43. Kathy Bell, 'The Midland Junction Railway Workshops, 1920 to 1939', *Studies in Western Australian History XI; Western Australia between the war 1919–1939*, ed. Jenny Gregory (June 1990), 35; Alfred Williams, *Life in a Railway Factory* (Stroud: Allan Sutton Publishing, 1986), 99.

p. 44-6. Ivan McMillan is quoted from 'Who Wants Moss?', unpublished personal memoir (2002), 1, Midland Workshops History Collection, SLWA Acc. no.

7625A/22. Other sources are Don Underdown, interviewed by Maxine Milne, January–February 2002, SLWA Acc. no. OH 3808/20; Don Manning, interviewed by Anthea Yap, 24 September 2003, SLWA Acc. no. OH3309; Bill Kirkham, conversation with the author, 25 March 2004; Lucy Taksa, 'Spatial practices and struggle over ground at Eveleigh Railway Workshops', in *Work. Organisation. Struggle. Papers from the seventh national labour history conference*. Held at the Australian National University, Canberra, 19–21 April 2001, eds Phil Griffiths and Rosemary Webb (Canberra: Australian Society for the Study of Labour History, Canberra Region Branch, 2001), 231. For a description of how the Beeching cuts affected railway footplate staff, see Robert Griffiths, *Driven by Ideals: a history of ASLEF* (London: ASLEF, 2005), 186–91.

Chapter 4

p. 47-8. Quotes are from Alfred Williams, *Life in a Railway Factory*, 243 and Stephen Smith interviewed by Maxine Milne, 24 February 2003, SLWA Acc. no. OH 3808/25.

p. 51. Michael Goff, interviewed by Bobbie Oliver for the East Perth Power Station Project, 24 January 2007, SLWA Acc. no. OH3595/40.

p. 52. Quoted from Jack Emery, 'Learning a Trade: Memories of anpprentice Turner and Iron Machinist, 29 January 1940 to 1 April 1945', *Papers in Labour History*, no. 25 (September 2001), 18, and Fred Cadwallader, interviewed by Ric McCracken, 2 July 2002, SLWA Acc. no. OH3248.

p. 53. Sources (apart from those mentioned previously) are E. Y. V. King, 'I've been working on the railroad', unpublished memoir donated to Midland Workshops History Project Collection, SLWA Acc. no. 7625A/22/King; Robert (Bob) Wells, interviewed by Dick Noyelle, 27 January 2003, SLWA Acc. no. OH3421; Ivan McMillan, 'Overalls 'n' Boots' – Memories of an Apprenticeship at the Workshops', *Papers in Labour History, no. 28: The Midland Railway Workshops Centenary Issue* (October 2004), 9; Alan Wahl, 'My Experiences at the WAGR Workshops, 1935 to 1960', *Papers in Labour History no. 25: The WAGR/ Westrail Midland Workshops* (September 2001), 2.

p. 54. Rod Quinn, 'The birth of my activism', *ibid*, 64. Geoff Hutchison, 'Memories of being an apprentice painter, 1944–50', Midland Workshops History Project Collection, SLWA Acc. no. 7625A/22/Hutchison.

p. 56. Kevin Wulff, interviewed by Bobbie Oliver, 31 January 2007.

Chapter 5

p. 60-1. Lenore Layman, 'Labour organisation: An industrial stronghold for unions', in *The Workshops*, 188–89; Lucy Taksa, "Pumping Life-Blood into

Politics and Place": Labour Culture and the Eveleigh Railway Workshops', *Labour History*, no. 79 (November 2000), 11-34. Jones is cited on 20.

p. 62-3. Sources that discuss the ALP split include Robert Murray, *The Split. Australian Labor in the fifties* (Sydney: Hale & Iremonger, 1970); Ross McMullin, *The Light on the Hill. The Australian Labor Party 1891–1991* (Melbourne: Oxford University Press, 1991), chapter 11, and Oliver, *Unity is Strength*, chapters 9 and 10. For the development of trades and labour councils in the nineteenth and twentieth centuries, see Bradon Ellem, Raymond Markey and John Shields, eds, *Peak Unions in Australia. Origins, Purpose, Power, Agency* (Sydney: The Federation Press, 2004), 161–72. For communist activity in Western Australia, see, for example, Bobbie Oliver and W. S. Latter, 'Spooks, Spies and Subversives! The Wartime Security Service', in *On the Homefront. Western Australia and World War II*, ed. Jenny Gregory (Nedlands: UWA Press, 1996), 176–85; Stuart Macintyre, *Militant. The life and times of Paddy Troy* (Sydney: Allen & Unwin, 1984). Macintyre (107) states that the WA results of the referendum to ban the CPA were 164,989 in favour, 134,497 against.

p. 63. The 1952 strike is discussed by Jan Archer, 'The 1952 Metal Trades Strike in Western Australia, a War of Attrition', *Papers in Labour History no. 25: The WAGR/Westrail Midland Workshops*, September 2001, 67–79; also Layman, 'Labour organisation', in *The Workshops*, 186–88. Anecotes about Jack Marks are from Jolly Read, *Marksy. The life of Jack Marks* (South Fremantle: Read Media, 1998), 61–62.

p. 65. Cathy Bridgen, 'Power and Space in the Victorian Trades Hall Council', in *Peak Unions in Australia*, 220. Iodine Annie is mentioned by Dave Hicks, interviewed by Katina Devril (14 September 2003) and several other interviewees.

p. 67. All quotes from various issues of *Unity*, in Annette & Duncan Cameron Papers, SLWA Acc. no. 4765A (MN 1504), Box 18, item 20. For the labourer sacked for breaching Workshops rules, see Ric McCracken, 'Work Culture', in *The Workshops*, 209. King's recollection is from his unpublished memoir, 'I've been working on the railroad', donated to Midland Workshops History Project Collection, SLWA Acc. no. 7625A/22/King. Sheridan is cited from *Mindful Militants*, 193.

p. 68-9. Marks' explanation of how he was employed at the Workshops is from Read, *Marksy*, 35; see also *Annual Reports* of Foreman Fitter, 1951; Foreman Boilermaker 1951, 1953, 1956; Foreman Paint Shop, 1944–45, in WAGR Papers, SROWA CONS 5267, WAS 1405, item 66/2841, various volume numbers. The *Government Railways Act 1904–1967*, By-law 84: Workshops Rules, nos 61 and 62. Copies held in WAGR Papers, SROWA, CONS 5267, WAS1403, item 1976/2799, vol 1. Dennis Day's recollection of his sackings is in a letter to Ric McCracken, n.d., Midland Workshops History Project Collection, SLWA Acc. no. 7625A/22/ Day. For an account of the Portnoy case, see Geoff Davis, 'The Pioneer Bookshop and *Portnoy's Complaint*', in *Radical Perth, Militant Fremantle*, eds Charlie Fox,

Bobbie Oliver and Lenore Layman (Perth: Black Swan Press, 2017, 153–59).

p. 71. For the Paul Robeson incident, see SRO: 66/2880, Volume 6, CME Joint Railways Unions Deputations, Marks to Britter (works manager), 29 November 1960. Robeson's concert was recalled by many Midland employees; see also Ann Curthoys, ' Paul Robeson's visit to Australia and Aboriginal activism, 1960' in *Passionate Histories: myth, memory and indigenous Australia*, eds, Frances Peters-Little, Ann Curthoys and John Docker (Canberra: ANU E Press, 2010), 17677.

Chapter 6

p. 73-4. The CD referred to is *The Westrail Workshops Oral History Interviews*, produced by Geraldine Harris and Mia Lindgren (Murdoch: Murdoch University, 2001). The term 'craft consciousness' is used in the manner of Sheridan, *Mindful Militants*, 57 and 155, to denote a perceived hierarchy of skills among the trades. Several interviewees commented on the extensive training given in a Workshops apprenticeship, as did, for example, Nicholas Dragicevich, interviewed by Sharleen Olsen, 26 April 2002, SLWA Acc. no.OH3297. Dragicevich is quoted from the same interview elsewhere. Lucas Pitsikas, interviewed by Gail O'Hanlon, 17 December 1997 and 7 January 1998, SLWA Acc. no. OH 2867. Pitsikas was a planner in the boiler shop; he became works manager in 1968, and CME from 1976 until 1980, when he retired.

p. 75. Steve Smith's comment on hierarchies is from his interview with Maxine Milne, 24 February 2003, SLWA Acc. no. OH 3808/25.

p. 76. The quotes from Don Underdown throughout this chapter are from his interview with Maxine Milne, January–February 2002, SLWA Acc. no. OH 3808/20.

p. 77. The table was compiled by the author from figures in the *Minutes of the Apprentices Application and Selection Board*, Westrail Workshops History Project Collection, SLWA Acc. 7652A/17 OSM.

p. 78-80. The information here is drawn from interviews with Dave Moir, Bob Wells, Bill Kirkham and Sindy Hunter.

p. 81. For the development of OH&S legislation in Western Australia, see Minutes of the Occupational Health & Safety (OH&S) Committee, in TLC Papers SLWA, MN 117711, Series 4442A/33 Occupational Health & Safety 1984–89. Moving the township of Wittenoom was discussed in *Western Australian Parliamentary Debates (WAPD)*, vol. 25, (1984), 1544. I received information on the TLC campaign from a conversation with retired MLA Judyth Watson on 30 January 2001. Graeme Bywater, interviewed by Nancy McKenzie, 17 December 2002, SLWA Acc.no. OH3424.

p. 83. 'Lost-time injury': when one person loses one 8-hour shift. Mae Jean

Parker, interviewed by Maxine Milne, 3 December 2002, SLWA Acc.no. OH3412.

Chapter 7

p. 85-8. The reference to privatisation is from Bobbie Oliver, 'The Impact of Union Amalgamation on Membership: An Australian Case Study', SAGE Open (July–September 2016), 1–8. Sources for the Australian Standard Garratt strike are Bobbie Oliver, 'The Australian Standard Garratt: the engine that brought down a government', *Journal of Transport History*, 33, no. 1 (June 2012), 21–41; Report of the Royal Commissioner, Justice Wolff, Royal Commission appointed to inquire into the Australian Standard Garratt Locomotive, 1946 [hereafter Wolff, *Report of the Garratt Royal Commission*, 1946], 56.

p. 88-9. For the formation of an independent trades and labour council in Western Australia, see Oliver, *Unity is Strength*. On the decline in union membership, see Malcolm Rimmer, 'Unions and Arbitration', in *The New Province for Law and Order. 100 years of Australian industrial Conciliation and Arbitration*, eds, Joe Isaac and Stuart Macintyre (Melbourne: Cambridge University Press, 2004), 294–303; Michael Crosby, *Power at Work. Rebuilding the Australian Union Movement* (Sydney: The Federation Press, 2005), 17ff. The quote, 'Permanency is now a myth' is from Report of the West Australian Locomotive Engine Drivers', Firemen's and Cleaners Union, WA Divisional Secretary to the 43rd Australian Council Meeting of the Australian Federated Union of Locomotive Enginemen, Launceston, 21–24, March 1988. The figures indicating the declining workforce are from Elliott, 'Derailed', 238, in *The Workshops*, and 'Total Employees', in file 'Details of Services made available to staff', Midland Workshops History Project, SLWA Acc. no. 7625A/5.

p. 90. For union power in the Pilbara, see Bradon Ellem, *From Deserts the Profits Come* (Perth: UWA Publishing, 2017). On the Accord from the ACTU point of view, see Bill Kelty, 'The Accord. Industrial Relations in the Trade Union Movement', in *The Hawke Government: A critical retrospective*, eds, Susan Ryan and Tony Bramston (Melbourne: Pluto Press Australia, 2003), 328 ff.

p. 91-2. On the Burke government and the Tripartite Council, see Rose Anne Graham, 'The Consensus Legacy: The Burke Government and the Trade Union Movement: 1983–1987', *Papers in Labour History no. 17*, (December 1996), 70–81; Oliver, *Unity is Strength*, 333. All references to David Heald's report are from David Heald, 'Privatisation and Public Sector Reform in Australia: Regaining Control of the Agenda', unpublished report, n.d., cited in Bobbie Oliver, 'A total anathema to Labor?' The privatisation debate in Western Australia in the 1980s', in *Work, employment and employment relations in an uneven patchwork world, Proceedings of the 27th AIRAANZ Conference, Esplanade Hotel, Fremantle, 6–8 February*, eds, A. Rainnie and P. Todd (Perth: AIRAANZ, Curtin University, UWA, 2013), 180–91(DVD).

p. 92-4. Peter Dowding is quoted from his letter to Stephen Smith (ALP State

Secretary), 25 July 1988, in Trades and Labour Council of WA Papers, SLWA Acc. 4442/114, 'Privatisation'. Rob Meecham is quoted from his letter to Bob Hawke, 21 March 1989, in TLCWA file 4442/114; Clive Brown and Richard Court are both cited in Oliver, *Unity is Strength*, 342–43.

p. 95. Peter Carty is quoted from his interview with Chelsea Gellard, 9 May 2003, Midland Railway Workshops History Project, SLWA Accession no. OH 3251, and with Mia Lindgren, extracts of which appear on the DVD *Midland Workshops Life*.

p. 96. Sindy Hunter, Robert Rowe and Kevin Mountain all appeared on the DVD *Midland Workshops Life*. Information on redundancies and transfers is from 'Closure of Midland Workshops – alphabetical listing of Midland Workshops staff showing those accepting redundancy package, redeployment to other government departments or transfer to other Westrail Divisions' in the file titled, 'Details of Services made available to staff', Midland Workshops History Project, SLWA Acc. 7625A/5. Examples of workers being directed into low-paid, low-skilled work are from Elliott, 'Derailed', 252, and *Midland Workshops Life*.

p. 97. Information on change management processes is from 'Proposal for Change Management Workshops for Westrail, Midland Unit' in file 'Details of Services made available to staff', n.d., Midland Workshops History Project, SLWA Acc. 7625A/5. The observation about the impact of privatisation is from Bobbie Oliver, 'The impact of privatisation on union membership: A Western Australian Case Study', *Economic and Labour Relations Review*, 25, no. 1 (March 2014), 28–46. There are numerous blogs, news items and comments on skills shortage in Australia. An example is Michael Taylor, 'Skills Shortage in Australia', posted on AI Group Blog, 6 February 2018. Taylor states that the 'technicians and trade workers grouping' was a 'key employment group' suffering skills shortages. This grouping included automotive and engineering trades workers and construction trades workers, who would once have been trained at large government facilities such as railway workshops. See blog.aigroup.com.au/skills-shortages-in-australia/, accessed 25 July 2018; see also ABC *News*, 20 July 2005.

p. 98-9. The RTBU's comment was accessed at rtbu-nat.asn.au/241.html on 14 September 2009. Unfortunately, the page is no longer available. For information on the numerical strength of unions, see RTBU, 'History', rtbu.org.au/a_short_history and en.wikipedia.org/wiki/Transport_Workers_Union_of_Australia; see also Transport Workers Union of Australia twu.com.au/about/; all accessed 25 July 2018; see also Crosby, *Power at Work*, 19. For comment on twenty-first century factory closures, see Andrew Beer et al. (2006), *An evaluation of the impact of retrenchment at Mitsubishi focussing on affected workers, their families and communities: implications for human services policies and practices*, Adelaide: Flinders University; see also Carrington Clarke (2017), 'Toyota and Holden factories to close; end of the line for auto workers', ABC *News* online, abc.net.au/news/2017-10-02/toyota-and-holden-factories-to-shut-down/9008312, accessed 30 July 2018.

Chapter 8

p. 106-7. Colin Divall is quoted from his paper 'Routes and Roots: Moving Beyond Australian Railways as Myth', *Historic Environment*, Vol. 21, No. 2 (July 2008), 25–31. For information on the impact of standard gauge rail on Western Australian railway crews, see Oliver, *The Locomotive Enginemen*, 311–13 (iBooks edition).
ABC *News*, 20 July 2005.

BIBLIOGRAPHY

'Addington Railway Workshops', accessed 28 April 2004 at embassy.orgn.nz/awsh3.htm.

Aplin, Graeme (2002), *Heritage. Identification, Conservation and Management* (Melbourne: Oxford University Press).

Archer, Jan (2001), 'The 1952 Metal Trades Strike in Western Australia: A War of Attrition', *Papers in Labour History, no. 25: WAGR/Westrail Midland Workshops*, (September), 67–79.

Barry, Kevin (1966), 'Labour Divided: The Garratt Strike of 1946', *Papers in Labour History*, no. 17 (December), 46–67.

Batterham, Linley (2006), 'Women munitions workers, 1943–45', in *The Workshops. A History of the Midland Government Railway Workshops*, eds Patrick Bertola and Bobbie Oliver (Nedlands: UWA Press), 128–43.

Beer, Andrew, et. al. (2006), *An evaluation of the impact of retrenchment at Mitsubishi focussing on affected workers, their families and communities: implications for human services policies and practices* (Adelaide: Flinders University, 2006).

Bell, Kathy (1990), 'The Midland Junction Railway Workshops, 1920 to 1939', *Studies in Western Australian History XI; Western Australia between the wars 1919–1939*, ed. J. Gregory (June), 29–42.

Bertola, Patrick (2008), 'Asbestos Exposure through the accounts of four workers at the former WAGR Workshops', and 'Chasing the "truths": asbestos exposure and information sites', in Patrick Bertola and Lenore Layman, eds, *Papers in Labour History*, no. 27 (November), 67–71.

Bertola, Patrick (2008), 'Exposure to asbestos at the Midland Workshops: documents and commentary' in *Papers in Labour History, Asbestos: Danger, Disease & Struggle*, no. 27, eds Lenore Layman and Geoff Davis (November), 33–50.

Bertola, Patrick (2008), 'Searching for "facts" on asbestos: labour history research via worldwide web', in *Papers in Labour History, Asbestos: Danger, Disease & Struggle*, no. 27, eds Lenore Layman and Geoff Davis (November), 67–71.

Bertola, Patrick & Oliver, Bobbie (2006), eds, *The Workshops. A History of the Midland Government Railway Workshops* (Nedlands: UWA Press).

Booth, A. L. & Satchell, S. E. (1994), 'Apprenticeships and Job Tenure', *Oxford Economic Papers*, 46, 676–95.

Bridgen, Cathy (2004), 'Power and Space in the Victorian Trades Hall Council', in *Peak Unions in Australia.Origins, Purpose, Power, Agency*, eds Bradon Ellem, Raymond Markey and John Shields (Sydney: The Federation Press), 219–35.

Bunt, Brogan (2004), *Midland Railway Workshops. An interactive oral history*, mcc.murdoch.edu.au/midland/. This website is no longer hosted by Murdoch University.

Bunt, Brogan (2002), 'New Media documentary', *Metro*, December.

Carney, Bernard (2002), 'The Midland Railway Workshops', track 9 from the CD *West*.

Clarke, Carrington (2017), 'Toyota and Holden factories to close; end of the line for auto workers', ABC *News* online at abc.net.au/news/2017-10-02/toyota-and-holden-factories-to-shut-down/9008312, accessed 30 July 2018.

Crosby, Michael (2005), *Power at Work. Rebuilding the Australian Union Movement* (Sydney: The Federation Press, 2005)

Curthoys, Ann (2010), 'Paul Robeson's visit to Australia and Aboriginal activism, 1960', in *Passionate Histories: myth, memory and indigenous australia*, eds Frances Peters-Little, Ann Curthoys and John Docker (Canberra: ANU E Press).

Davis, Geoff, 'The Pioneer Bookshop and *Portnoy's Complaint*', in *Radical Perth, Militant Fremantle*, eds, Charlie Fox, Bobbie Oliver and Lenore Layman (Perth: Black Swan Press), 153–59.

Divall, Colin (2008), 'Routes and Roots: Moving Beyond Australian Railways as Myth', *Historic Environment*, 21, no. 2 (July), 25–31.

Docherty, J. C. (1983), 'Hollis, Robert (1851–1937)', *Australian Dictionary of Biography*, National Centre of Biography, Australian National University (accessed online 2 August 2018).

Ellem, Bradon (2017), *From Deserts the Profits Come* (Nedlands: UWA Publishing).

Elliott, Lyla (2006), '"Derailed'-": The closure of the Midland Workshops', in *The Workshops. A History of the Midland Government Railway Workshops*, eds Patrick Bertola and Bobbie Oliver (Nedlands: UWA Press), 235–58.

Ellis, Nic and Smyth, Chris (2004), *Midland railway workshops* (Osborne Park: St George Books).

Emery, Jack (2001), 'Learning a Trade. Memories of an Apprentice Turner and Iron Machinist, 29 January 1940–1, April 1945', *Papers in Labour History no. 25: The WAGR/Westrail Midland Workshops* (September), 10–26.

Farr, David and Associates (2003), *Feasibility Study, (David Farr and Associates, Perth, 2003)*.

Fox, Charlie (2006), 'Work Organisation', in *The Workshops. A History of the Midland Government Railway Workshops*, eds Patrick Bertola and Bobbie Oliver (Nedlands: UWA Press), 81–105.

Government of Western Australia, *Railways Act 1904–1967*, by-law 84: Workshops Rules, Nos 61 and 62, WAGR Papers, SROWA, CONS 5267, WAS1403, item 1976/2799, vol 1.

Graham, Rose Anne (1996), 'The Consensus Legacy: The Burke Government and the Trade Union Movement: 1983–1987', *Papers in Labour History no. 17* (December), 70–81.

Gregory, Jenny (2008), 'Obliterating History? The Transformation of Inner City Industrial Suburbs', *Australian Historical Studies*, 39, 91–106.

Griffiths, Robert (2005), *Driven by Ideals: A history of ASLEF* (London: ASLEF), 186–91.

Harris, Geraldine and Lindgren, Mia (2001), producers, *The Westrail Workshops Oral History Interviews*, Murdoch University, SLWA Acc VDA232.

Harris, Jennifer, ed. (2009), *Foreigners, Secret Artefacts of Industrialism* (Perth: Black Swan Press).

Hartley, Richard G (2006), 'Midland Junction Workshops: Mechanical engineering and Government policies', in *The Workshops. A History of the Midland Government Railway Workshops*, eds Patrick Bertola and Bobbie Oliver (Nedlands: UWA Press), 106–27.

Heritage and Conservation Professionals (2001), *Draft Heritage Strategy for Midland Central Redevelopment Area*, prepared for the Midland Redevelopment Authority, Strategy Papers Nos 1, 2 and 3.

High, Steven and Lewis, David W. (2007), *Corporate Wasteland. The Landscape and Memory of Deindustrialisation* (Ithaca: Cornell University Press).

Highfield, Ann (2006), 'Midland, the suburb', in *The Workshops. A History of the Midland Government Railway Workshops*, eds Patrick Bertola and Bobbie Oliver (Nedlands: UWA Press), 39–60.

Hobsbawm, E. J. (1967) 'Trade Union History', in *Economic History Review*, 20, no. 2 (August), 358–64.

Hobsbawm, E. J. (1985), 'The "New Unionism" Reconsidered', in *The Development of Trade Unionism in Great Britain and Germany, 1880–1914*, eds W. J. Mommsen & H.-G. Husung (London: George Allen & Unwin), 13–32.

Kelty, Bill (2003), 'The Accord. Industrial Relations in the Trade Union Movement' in eds S. Ryan and T. Bramston, *The Hawke Government: A critical retrospective* (Melbourne: Pluto Press Australia).

King, E. Y. V. 'I've been working on the railroad', unpublished memoirs donated to Midland Workshops History Project Collection, SLWA Acc. 7625A/22/King.

Layman, Lenore (2006), 'Labour organisation: An industrial stronghold for unions', in *The Workshops. A History of the Midland Government Railway Workshops*, eds Patrick Bertola and Bobbie Oliver (Nedlands: UWA Press), 172–95.

Lindgren, Mia (2004), director and producer, *Midland Workshops Life* (DVD).

Macintyre, Stuart (1984), *Militant. The life and times of Paddy Troy* (Sydney: Allen & Unwin).

Macintyre, Stuart (1998), 'Basic Wage', in *The Oxford Companion to Australian History*, eds Graeme Davison, John Hirst and Stuart Macintyre (Oxford: Oxford University Press), 62.

Markey, Ray and Nixon, Shirley (2004), 'Peak Unionism in the Illawarra', in *Peak Unions in Australia. Origins, Purpose, Power, Agency*, eds Bradon Ellem, Raymond Markey and John Shields (Sydney: The Federation Press), 161–72.

Marquis-Kyle, Peter and Walker, Meredith (1992), *The Illustrated Burra Charter* (Sydney: ICOMOS).

McCracken, Ric (2006), 'Work Culture', in *The Workshops. A History of the Midland Government Railway Workshops*, eds Patrick Bertola and Bobbie Oliver (Nedlands: UWA Press), 199–214.

McCracken, Ric (2002), 'Planning for a State Rail Heritage Centre at the Midland Workshops', unpublished discussion paper, Midland Workshops History Project, SLWA Acc no. 7625A/22/McCracken.

McMillan, Ivan (2004), 'Overalls 'n' Boots – Memories of an Apprenticeship at the Workshops', *Papers in Labour History*, no. 28 (October), 5–11.

McMillan, Ivan (2002), 'Who Wants Moss?', unpublished memoir, Midland Workshops History Collection, SLWA Acc no. 7625A/22/McMillan.

McMullin, Ross (1991), *The Light on the Hill. The Australian Labor Party 1891–1991* (Melbourne: Oxford University Press).

Metropolitan Redevelopment Authority (2017), *Midland Heritage Interpretation Strategy*, Appendix 3, 'Midland Railway Workshops Interpretation', accessed 31 July 2018 at cdn.mra.wa.gov.au/production/documents-media/documents/midland/file/midland-heritage-interpretation-strategy.

Midland Redevelopment Authority (2000), *Draft Concept Plan*.

Midland Redevelopment Authority (2003), *Concept Planning for State Railway Heritage Centre Tender Brief*.

Midland Redevelopment Authority (2005), *The First Five Years 2000–2005*, accessed 31 July 2017 at cdn.mra.wa.gov.au/production/documents-media/documents/midland/file/the-first-five-years-2000-2005.pdf.

Midland Redevelopment Authority (2009), 'Planning – Helena Precinct'.

Midland Workshops History Project Collection, SLWA Acc. MN 2758, 7625A, 8921A.

Minutes of the Apprentices Application and Selection Board, Midland Workshops History Project Collection, SLWA Acc. 7625A/17 OSM.

Minutes of the Industrial Training Advisory Council (ITAC), 8 April 1987, in WAGR Papers, SROWA Cons 5692, item 7140/87.

Minutes of the Occupational Health & Safety (OH&S) Committee, in Trades and Labor Council Papers SLWA, MN 117711, Series 4442A/33 Occupational Health & Safety 1984-89.

Murray, Robert (1970), *The Split. Australian Labor in the Fifties* (Sydney: Hale & Iremonger).

NCVER, 'Australian Apprenticeships: Research at a glance', accessed 28 November 2003 at ncver.edu.au/research/proj2/mk0008/milestone.htm.

Oliver, Bobbie (2003), *Unity is Strength. A history of the Australian Labor Party and the Trades and Labor Council in Western Australia, 1899–1999* (Perth: API Books).

Oliver, Bobbie (2003), '"Transforming labour" at the Westrail Workshops, Midland WA, 1940s and 1990s', in *Transforming Labour. Work, Workers, Struggle and Change, Proceedings of the Eighth National Labour History Conference, Brisbane, 3–5 October 2003*, eds Bradley Bowden and John Kellett (Brisbane: Brisbane Labour History Association), 247–52.

Oliver, Bobbie (2004), 'The Formation and Role of an Independent Trades and Labor Council in Western Australia', in *Peak Unions in Australia. Origins, Purpose, Power, Agency*, eds Bradon Ellem, Raymond Markey and John Shields (Sydney: The Federation Press), 116–32.

Oliver, Bobbie (2006), 'The Apprenticeship System at the Workshops', in *The Workshops. A History of the Midland Government Railway Workshops*, eds Patrick Bertola and Bobbie Oliver (Nedlands: UWA Press), 63–80.

Oliver, Bobbie (2007), '"They can't take a trade off you" – varying perceptions of job security over 50 years at the Midland Government Railway Workshops', in *The Time of Their Lives: the Eight Hour Day and Working Life*, eds Julie Kimber and Peter Love (Sydney: Australian Society for the Study of Labour History),

153–68.

Oliver, Bobbie (2011), 'The Australian Standard Garratt: the engine that brought down a government', *Journal of Transport History*, 33, no. 1 (June), 21–41.

Oliver, Bobbie (2013), '"A total anathema to Labor?" The privatisation debate in Western Australia in the 1980s', in *Work, employment and employment relations in an uneven patchwork world, Proceedings of the 27th AIRAANZ Conference, Esplanade Hotel, Fremantle, 6–8 February,* (CD), eds A. Rainnie and P. Todd (Perth: AIRAANZ with Curtin University and UWA), 180–91.

Oliver, Bobbie (2014), 'The impact of privatisation on union membership: A Western Australian Case Study', *Economic and Labour Relations Review*, 25, no. 1 (March), 28–46.

Oliver, Bobbie (2016a), 'The Impact of Union Amalgamation on Membership: An Australian Case Study', SAGE Open (July–September), 1–8, DOI: 10.1177/2158244016658086.

Oliver, Bobbie (2016b) *The Locomotive Enginemen. A history of the West Australian Locomotive Engine Drivers', Firemen's and Cleaners' Union* (Perth: Black Swan Press).

Oliver, Bobbie and Latter, W. S. (1996), 'Spooks, Spies and Subversives! The Wartime Security Service', in *On the Homefront. Western Australia and World War II*, ed. Jenny Gregory (Nedlands: UWA Pres), 176–85.

Oliver, Bobbie and Reeves, Andrew (2003), 'Crossing Disciplinary Boundaries: Labour History and Museum Studies', *Labour History*, no. 85 (November), 1–7.

Palm, Dawn (2001), 'Creativity at the Workshops', *Papers in Labour History no. 25: The WAGR/Westrail Midland Workshops* (September), 50–62.

Payne, Jonathan (2000), *National Skills Task Force Issues Final Report*, Eurofound: the European Foundation for the improvement of living and working conditions, accessed 24 September 2018 at eurofound.europa.eu/publications/article/2000/national-skills-task-force-issues-final-report.

Payne, Jonathan (1999), 'The changing meaning of skill and its implications for UK vocational education and training policy', Eurofound: the European Foundation for the improvement of living and working conditions, accessed 24 September 2018 at eurofound.europa.eu/publications/article/1999/the-changing-meaning-of-skill-and-its-implications-for-uk-vocational-education-and-training-policy.

Payne, Jonathan, 'Government seeks to expand and revitalise modern apprenticeships' (2002), Eurofound: the European Foundation for the improvement of living and working conditions, accessed 24 September 2018 at eurofound.europa.eu/lv/publications/article/2002/government-seeks-to-expand-and-revitalise-modern-apprenticeships

Peel, Robyn (2001), 'Management of Industrial Injury and Work-place safety in the WAGR Midland Workshops (from the early days at Midland Junction until the late 1950s)', *Papers in Labour History no. 25: The WAGR/Westrail Midland Workshops* (September), 80–100.

Quinn, Rod, 'The birth of my activism' (2001), *Papers in Labour History no. 25: The WAGR/Westrail Midland Workshops* (September), 63–66.

Read, Jolly (1998), *Marksy. The life of Jack Marks*, (Fremantle: Read Media).

Report of the Royal Commissioner, Justice Wolff, Royal Commission appointed to inquire into the Australian Standard Garratt Locomotive, 1946, accessed 8 August 2014 at parliament.wa.gov.au/intranet/libpages.nsf/WebFiles.

INDEX

accidents 29, 55, 82, 83, 86, 98, 111
Addington Railway Workshops (Christchurch, NZ) 33, 45, 119
Amalgamated Engineering Union (AEU) 38, 50, 61, 62–3, 65, 68, 88, 111
apprenticeships 31, 41–3, 44, 57, 73–4, 78–80, 112, 120, 123, 124
asbestos 30, 31, 55, 71, 81, 101, 119, 120
Associated Society of Locomotive Engineers and Firemen, UK (ASLEF) 40, 46, 113, 121
Australian Labor Party (ALP) 2, 13, 59, 61–3, 65, 67, 72, 88, 90, 92–3, 111, 113, 116, 122, 123
Australian Standard Garratt locomotive (ASG) 85, 86–8, 107, 116, 125
Australian Workers' Union (AWU) 39, 61
Bell, Kathy 43–4, 62, 112, 119
Bethlehem Steel Works (Pennsylvania) 16–17
blacksmiths 44, 48, 75–79, 79, 81–2
Block 1 7, 14, 17, 19, 20, 22, 24, 28, 64, 101–2
Block 2 7, 28
Block 3 7, 13, 18, 28, 59
boiler shop 2, 23, 41, 64, 74, 95, 115
boilermakers 2, 29, 31, 41, 44, 48, 54, 62–3, 75, 77, 81, 95, 114
Bristow Stagg, Phillip 65
British diaspora 6, 34, 35, 40, 46, 47
Brown, Clive (TLCWA state secretary) 93, 117
Burke, Brian (WA premier, 1983–88) 90–1, 116, 120

Burra Charter 5, 7, 73, 109, 122
Bywater, Graeme 81, 115
Cadwallader, Fred 52–3, 64, 113
Carty, Peter 30, 31, 32, 95, 96, 111, 117
chief mechanical engineer (CME)'s office 7–9, 18, 27, 58, 64, 86, 101, 102, 114, 115
closed shop 39, 43, 46, 63, 88–9
Coal Dam 27, 101, 102
Coleman, Jack 63–4, 66, 71–2
Communist Party of Australia (CPA) 59, 61–3, 65, 69, 71–2, 114
communists 59, 61–68, 71–2, 88
Court, Richard (WA premier, 1993–2001) 13, 31, 93, 95, 96, 101, 117
craft status 44, 76
cupola, the 29
David Farr and Associates' Feasibility Study 20–1, 110, 121
Day, Dennis 69, 114
Democratic Labour Party (DLP) 65, 67–8
dieselisation 44–5, 76, 89
Divall, Colin 106-7, 118, 120
Double the Margins campaign (1952) 63–4
Draft Concept Plan 20, 110, 123
Dragicevich, Nick 80, 81, 115
East Perth Power Station 12, 49, 54, 56, 58, 113
Emery, Jack 42, 52, 112, 121
equal opportunity 80
Eveleigh Workshops 17, 24, 35, 45, 61, 90, 113
fatalities 29, 49, 55, 111
fitters, mechanical and electrical 29, 44, 53, 55, 56, 59, 65, 75, 77, 78, 96, 114
flagpole 8, 14, 18–19, 28, 58, 64, 69, 71
flagpole meetings 19, 28, 66, 69, 71
footplate staff 39, 41, 113
Forrest and Spiers 20, 21, 110
foundry 7, 8, 11, 22–3, 27, 29, 30, 51–3, 58, 64, 76, 101–2

Garratt strike 87–8, 116, 119
Gayton, Patrick 31, 65, 111
Goff, Michael 51, 54–5, 113
Hall, Susan 26, 32
Hawke, Albert (Bert) (premier, Western Australia, 1953–59) 71
Hawke, Robert (Bob) (prime minister, 1983–91) 88, 90, 92, 93, 116, 117, 122
Heald, David (report, 1986) 91–2, 116
Heritage Council of Western Australia 8, 13, 21, 25
Heritage Strategy (Heritage and Conservation Professionals, 2001) 14, 18, 20, 26, 110, 121
Hicks, Dave 65, 114
High, Steven 15, 110
History Project, The (see also Midland Workshops History Project)
Hollis, Robert 40, 112, 120
Howard, John (prime minister, 1996–2007) 92, 95, 98, 99
Humphrey, B. 29
Hunter, Sindy 80, 96, 115, 117
Hutchison, Geoff 54, 113
initiation 30, 34, 47–58, 83, 106
Joint Railways Union Committee 67, 115
Kenworthy, G. A. 29
King, Edward 67
Kirkham, Bill 44, 80, 102, 113, 115
Labour History Society (ASSLH) 2, 8, 9, 12, 13, 20, 110
Lacey, Norm 67, 69
Liberal Party (WA) 90–1, 93–4
Locomotive Engine Drivers', Firemen's and Cleaners' Union (LED) 39, 40–1, 85, 112, 116, 124
Machinery Preservation Society 22, 23
Manning, Don 66, 82–3, 113
Marks, Jack 18, 59–60, 63–72, 102, 114, 115, 124
Master of Apprentices 44, 80
McCracken, Ric 10, 13–14, 20, 26, 32, 110, 113, 114, 122
McDougall, Neil 29, 55, 111

McMillan, Ivan 44, 53, 112, 113, 122

McNamara, Leo 65, 69

Meecham, Rob 93, 117

Metropolitan Redevelopment Authority (MetRA) 3, 8, 20, 22, 23–4, 25, 58, 102, 104, 106, 108, 110, 111, 122

Midland 1–3, 5, 6–12, 14, 15, 44,

Midland Junction 6, 39, 62, 111, 112, 119, 121, 125

Midland Heritage Interpretation Strategy 3, 8, 20, 22–4, 25, 58, 102, 104–6, 108, 111, 122

Midland Railway Workshops (WAGR Workshops; Railway Workshops) 1, 5–8, 16–17, 21, 25, 27, 34, 35–8, 41, 42, 43, 46, 47–58, 59–62, 71, 72, 73, ¬83, 85–6, 88–9, 93, 95, 99¬–100, 101, 102, 103, 106, 109, 110, 111, 112, 113, 114, 117, 119, 120, 121, 123, 124

Midland Redevelopment Authority (MRA) 3, 8, 9, 11, 12, 13, 17, 19–22, 24, 25, 31, 32, 58, 101, 110, 111, 121, 123

Midland Workshops History Project (The History Project) 6, 9–13, 15, 16, 17, 18, 20–1, 23, 25, 28, 30, 31–4, 49, 55, 95, 103, 104, 105, 107, 109, 110, 113, 114, 115, 116, 117, 122, 123

Moir, Dave 79, 82, 115

Montgomery, Ray 104, 107

Mountain, Kevin 54, 96, 117

Munitions Annexe (see also Shell Annexe) 7, 13, 17

National Railway Museum (York, UK) 23

new unionism 37, 39, 111, 122

occupational health and safety (OHS) 57, 66, 81–4, 91, 115, 122

O'Connor, Charles Yelverton 27, 102

Open Day 8–9, 11, 21, 105, 110

paint shop 51, 53, 58, 114

Parker, Mae Jean 54, 57, 58, 80, 83, 115

pattern shop 8, 14, 22, 23, 101

peace memorial 7, 8, 14, 18, 58 64, 101

Peanut King, The 30, 50, 51–3, 58

Pitsikas, Lucas (Luke) 69, 74, 80, 115

power house 8, 14, 22, 101

pranks 47, 49–51, 54, 56, 58, 83
Prices and Incomes Accord (Accord, The) 90–1, 116, 122
privatisation 8, 34, 46, 85–6, 89–95, 98, 116, 117, 124
Quinn, Rod 54, 59, 113, 125
Rail Heritage Interpretive Centre (Interpretive Centre) 2–3, 15, 16, 20-1, 24, 32,105, 107
rail heritage centre 2, 3, 8, 11, 14, 19–24, 101, 110, 122
Rail Heritage WA 19, 22–4
Rail, Tram and Bus Union (RTBU) 98, 99, 110, 117
Railway Historical Society Western Australia 19 (see also Rail Heritage WA)
Red Square 18–19, 28, 59¬–60, 64–5
redundancy 96–7, 117
Robeson, Paul 11, 70–1, 114, 115, 120
Rowe, Robert 96, 117
safety officer 66, 82–3
Sanmor Consulting 20, 110
Shell Annexe (see also Munitions Annexe) 101
Sheridan, Tom 38, 50, 62, 68, 111, 114, 115
Smith, Stephen (Steve) 44, 48, 49, 51, 57, 75, 113, 115, 116
soil contamination 16, 101
steam locomotives 5, 23, 27, 44, 74
STEAM Museum (Swindon, UK) 3, 17, 19, 23, 26, 111,
strikes 37–8, 40, 62, 63, 68, 71, 85, 87–8
Swindon Workshops (UK) 36, 44
Taksa, Lucy 15, 17, 45, 61, 110, 113
timekeeper's office 2, 7, 8, 14–16, 20, 32, 101
Trades and Labor Council of Western Australia (TLC or TLCWA) 38, 61, 88, 90–4,111, 116, 117
Under the Lap, Over the Fence (exhibition, 2004) 11, 21
Underdown, Don 76–7, 78–9, 113, 115
Unity 67–71, 111, 114, 116, 117, 123
Wadham, Ron 1, 66, 109
Wahl, Alan 53–4, 113
Wells, Bob 53, 79, 113, 115

West Australian Amalgamated Society of Railway Employees (WAASRE) 39, 62–3, 67, 72

Western Australian Government Railways (WAGR) 1, 5–8, 25, 27, 34, 35, 39, 41, 49, 86, 88, 102, 109, 110, 112, 113, 114, 119, 121, 123, 124, 125

Westrail (formerly WAGR) 49, 80, 82, 89, 96, 97, 102, 110, 113, 114, 115, 117, 119, 121, 123, 124, 125

workers' wall 3, 17–18, 26, 104, 106

Workshops closure 19, 26, 30–1, 80, 84, 97, 98, 101

Workshops rules 67, 69, 114, 121

Wulff, Kevin 56, 113

Red Swan Series
WESTERN AUSTRALIAN RADICAL LABOUR HISTORY AND POLITICS

The Red Swan series in radical Western Australian labour history and politics, published by Interventions, brings to life stories from the workers' movement and social movements that need to be told. It offers a perspective on the state's history and politics that challenges the status quo.

Series Editor: Alexis Vassiley

FORTHCOMING TITLE:

Radical Perth Militant Fremantle
Edited by Charlie Oliver, Bobbie Oliver and Lenore Layman
Updated version with five new chapters
Anticipated publication date: October 2019

www.ingramcontent.com/pod-product-compliance
Lightning Source LLC
Chambersburg PA
CBHW070430010526
44118CB00014B/1982